EXECUTIVE DEVELOPMENT

A Strategy for Corporate Competitiveness

James F. Bolt

1817

Harper & Row, Publishers, New York
BALLINGER DIVISION

Grand Rapids, Philadelphia, St. Louis, San Francisco
London, Singapore, Sydney, Tokyo

Copyright © 1989 by Ballinger Publishing Company. All rights reserved.
No part of this publication may be reproduced, stored in a retrieval system, or transmitted in any form or by any means, electronic, mechanical,
photocopy, recording or otherwise, without the prior written consent of
the publisher.

International Standard Book Number: 0–88730–274–2

Library of Congress Catalog Card Number: 89–6813

Printed in the United States of America

Library of Congress Cataloging-in-Publication Data

Bolt, James F.
  Executive development.

  Includes index.
  1. Executives—Training of. I. Title.
HD38.2.B65 1989   658.4′ 07124   89–6813
ISBN 0–88730–274–2

89 90 91 HC 9 8 7 6 5 4 3 2 1

CONTENTS

LIST OF FIGURES

PREFACE

My goal in writing this book is to show CEO's and other executives how executive development can be used to help achieve strategic objectives. The idea for this book has been percolating in my mind for about a decade. When I assumed responsibility for executive education at Xerox Corporation in the late 1970s, I was immediately struck by the lack of published material. To be sure, there was a plethora of articles and books on training. There was even a good deal on management training, but virtually nothing on how leading American corporations go about educating and developing their very senior executives. That seemed to me to be a curious gap, and one which I determined I would someday help to close. This book helps fulfill that promise.

It was not until I had left Xerox in 1982 to start my own company—Executive Development Associates (EDA)—that I began to understand why the literature in my chosen field was so underdeveloped. The reason was deceptively simple: there was very little to write about.

Back in the 1970s and into the early 1980s, only a tiny handful of companies were seriously trying to educate their executives. Even among those who were, it was a rarity to find an executive development function that was professionally managed and integrated into the mainstream of corporate life. Executive education was typically seen as a "nice-to-do" activity, not as an essential thread in the fabric of a corporation's purpose and strategy.

All that has changed dramatically. More and more companies—many of them featured in this book—have come to the realization that the development and education of their senior executives is a key ingredient to their financial and marketplace health. Today, not only is there enough to write about but there is also a compelling *need* to collect this information and share it.

I say that there is a compelling need to do so because of the changing nature of the American corporation. Although we don't like to admit it and seldom talk about it, most American corporations operated as pseudo-monopolies throughout most of the twentieth century. Companies like Xerox and IBM did so because their technological innovations made them the dominant forces in their industries. Companies like AT&T did so partly because they operated under the protection of government regulation. Even in industries that we think of as being competitive—the automotive example comes easily to mind—a few companies dominated markets so huge that these companies could set their own rules. Also, the U.S. marketplace was so big and lucrative, there was little concern for the global marketplace.

No more. The onslaught of global competition, coupled with the trend toward government deregulation, has propelled virtually every major corporation into an intensely competitive environment. Many of them characterize their predicament as nothing short of a fight for their very survival. In that type of situation, every corporate function is quickly seen as either part of the problem or part of the solution. To its credit, the executive development function in some corporate settings has become part of the solution.

Most of this book reflects my experience as a consultant in executive development, working primarily with leading North American companies. Many of the companies described are clients.

In part I of this book, I talk about the changing nature of executive development. My firm has been documenting trends in executive education since 1983—trends toward more seriousness, more results-oriented education, more involvement of the chief executive officer. A corollary to these trends has been a shift in the methods used to deliver education to senior executives. There is, for example, less emphasis on lectures and case studies and more emphasis on hands-on, experiential types of learning.

Several companies have successfully used executive education as part of the complex process of managing organizational change. In Part II, I use General Electric—a unique enterprise on virtually everyone's list of best-managed companies—as an example. The reader will see how GE has used its overall management education process and its Management Development Institute to both lead and support change in the quarter-century. This part of the book also chronicles how Xerox Corporation used executive education to help communicate and implement its new strategic direction.

Part III covers two case studies of companies that have used executive education in very different ways to respond to the threat and the opportunity of global competition. In Part IV, I examine the executive education strategies born out of the necessities of deregulation of the telecommunications industry.

Both chapters in Part V deal with a single company—Weyerhaeuser. The forest products giant has been in the forefront of a return to making the customer king—the raison d'etre of the corporate enterprise. In the first chapter, we see how Weyerhaeuser used executive education to engineer a massive transformation and culture change. The other chapter takes an in-depth look at how Weyerhaeuser also used executive education to listen to its customer and to help its executives understand that the corporation must be driven by the forces of the marketplace.

Part VI covers leadership—the type of visionary, dynamic leadership that American corporations need to compete successfully in the global economy. My experience has been that leadership can indeed be taught. The chapter on General Foods is one example of how it can be done.

I conclude the book with a personal memorandum to our nation's CEOs. My message is simple. Executive education can help keep our corporations strong and competitive, but it can do so only with the proactive help and leadership of the CEO. Ultimately, it is they who must decide how best to use this newly discovered tool.

One last word. I would be remiss if I did not thank all of my clients and other friends in executive education at leading corporations and consulting firms around the country and all of my associates at Executive Development Associates. Their work inspired me to write this book and helped make it possible to complete it. They have my admiration and appreciation.

MEETING THE CHALLENGES OF THE 1990s

1 FORCES FOR CHANGE IN EXECUTIVE DEVELOPMENT

As even the casual observer of today's business scene can attest, large corporations are locked in battles for their very survival. The reasons vary. For some, it is the march of global competition into markets once dominated by the United States. For others, it is the impact of the Reagan years and the push toward deregulation and a freer economy. For still others, it is a court decree that forces them to divest themselves of major operations, which, in effect, become rivals in the marketplace.

But whatever the reason for struggling in today's business environments, the effect is the same: increased competition. Fully one-third of the Fortune 500 in 1970 have ceased to exist in 1988. Many that have continued in business have done so only after flirting with bankruptcy or merger.

Such a failure rate is not surprising, however, considering that the competitive marketplace—both domestic and international—keeps changing at a dramatic rate. Once fierce competitors now enter into joint ventures. New competitors keep appearing on the scene. Weak national economies—such as South Korea's—suddenly become commercial juggernauts.

In addition, the leverage of technology is declining as technology becomes less and less proprietary and, therefore, available to several competitors in the same market. A corporation can no longer rely solely on a technology as its exclusive ace-in-the-hole.

And if marketplaces weren't turbulant enough already, volatility in the world's money markets has increased the level of uncertainty and made strategic planning both more complex and more tentative.

The harsh realities of this new competitive environment have dictated new rules for corporate managements. They have been forced to downsize their companies, to streamline operations, to make their management more flexible, to rethink and revamp their strategic direction, and to become more focused and disciplined in their implementation of strategies.

Consequently, CEOs have examined every department and every function with one question in mind: "How can this unit and its employees help the company become more productive, more cost-effective, and more competitive?" No stone has been left unturned in this quest.

As one CEO told me:

> I can't afford to have anyone on board who is not pulling his or her own weight. We have to think of everyone as a direct employee and a contributor to the bottom line. If you're not part of the solution, you're part of the problem. And if you're part of the problem, I either have to make you part of the solution or we have to part company. That may seem hard-nosed, but I have to think that way in order to remain competitive, provide value to my customers and shareholders, and protect the jobs of my employees. It's really that simple.

In a 1988 study of corporate executive development efforts, Lyman W. Porter of the University of California at Irvine and Lawrence E. McKibbin of the University of Oklahoma concluded that it was a serious mistake for corporations to put other needs ahead of development. Executive development was judged a necessity to help top people with strategic or "big picture" thinking. Porter commented, "You can't run businesses like you did in the 1940s."

THE EVOLUTION OF
EXECUTIVE DEVELOPMENT

My firm, Executive Development Associates, has been tracking major industrywide trends in executive and management training and development since 1983. A conclusion of our first major study that I reported in the *Harvard Business Review* (November/December, 1985, p. 168) was "leading corporations are approaching the training and development of their top executives in a fundamentally different way than they did in the past."

We discovered in our survey of Fortune 500 companies that "the shift is a return to basics—training that is more results oriented, programs that are aimed at implementing business strategies and achieving corporate objectives." Among the principal survey findings were these:

- Senior executives had begun to play a more directive and proactive role in shaping management and executive development courses and curricula.
- The demand for greater productivity, the threat of worldwide competition, and the recognition of the need for fundamental corporate change had led to a greater demand for management training and development at the very highest levels of corporate America.

As a result, corporate giants—including the likes of Xerox, Motorola, Federated Department Stores, and General Foods—had already developed and implemented training programs aimed exclusively at their senior executives.

These programs were focused on implementing new corporate strategies that would improve financial performance. As such, these and other corporate programs had begun to break new ground. Companies using them were taking management training and development out of the closet and moving it to center stage in their strategic planning. We concluded that this new blend of "hard-hitting, business oriented content with an external focus may be the wave of the future."

Rapid Change from 1983 to 1986

That prediction was, if anything, understated. The changes that were only dim shadows in 1983 began to take on sharper definition, and much faster than we anticipated. In order to update and validate our 1983 survey, EDA conducted a second survey in 1986. Senior executives responsible for management training and development were asked a variety of questions about what had been happening in their corporations and in their functions over the previous three to five years and about what they expected would happen over the next three to five years.

Major findings of the 1986 survey included the following:

- Changes in business strategy and the need to implement these strategies with precision had become a stronger force in shaping management and executive training and development.

- The role of senior executives—including more and more chief executive officers—in the direction, design, and implementation of management training and development continued to expand.
- There was a significant increase in the amount of training—particularly for middle managers and executives.
- Internal, customized courses had replaced "off-the-shelf" and university-originated courses as the primary source of middle management and executive training and development.

Perhaps most revealing was a dramatic increase between 1983 and 1986 in programs related to formulating and implementing strategy, particularly courses aimed at enhancing global competitiveness. A driving force for this, of course, was the growing realization that Japan was winning the battle for global industrial supremacy.

One chief executive officer we interviewed at the time put it this way:

> The handwriting is on the wall and the message is clear. When I got out of high school, the Japanese accounted for only 2 percent of the world's economy. Now it's 10 percent and growing. And you know where their growth is coming from? The United States. We're in a fight for survival and we need all the help we can get. Management training and development has an important—even essential—role to play. We'd be crazy not to use it.

Our 1986 survey showed that this attitude was steadily spreading. With their management training programs more focused on strategy, productivity, leadership, and global competition, these senior executives were putting more emphasis on application: what is learned in the classroom should be used back on the job.

Executive Development in 1988

Early in 1988, we conducted our third major survey of a cross-section of Fortune 500 companies. Nearly fifty corporations participated. About half were manufacturing companies, and the rest included service, retail, financial, and telecommunications firms. Revenues of the companies participating in the survey ranged from $1 billion to $20 billion a year, and the number of their employees ranged from 10,000 to 175,000.

Unlike the first two surveys, which covered both management and executive development, our 1988 survey was concerned exclusively with the development of executives and those high-potential managers destined to become executives. For the first time, *development* was defined as any activity that broadens executives' knowledge and experience and helps them enhance their capabilities. A *high-potential manager* was defined as an individual who has been identified as possessing the potential to fill an executive-level position in the future. *Executives* were defined as one or more of the following:

- The chairman of the board, the chief executive officer, the chief operating officer, or the president
- All elected officers
- Corporate vice presidents (including functional heads)
- Heads/presidents of groups, divisions, business units, or profit centers and their direct reports
- All people included in the executive compensation program

The 1988 survey confirms that executive development is growing in importance and influence. Figure 1–1 summarizes our 1988 findings. What we found is that the single most powerful and pervasive impetus behind executive education is the worldwide competitive environment, which has had a tremendous impact on virtually all large corporations. This impact is felt in three main ways:

- To survive in the new environment, corporations must set new *standards* for productivity, quality, and cost-effectiveness.
- Many corporations are changing their business *strategies* in an effort to become more productive and competitive.
- Many companies are finding that their corporate *cultures,* which served them well in the past, must be totally revamped to incorporate new values, new management styles, and the new strategies required for success in the hard realities of the global marketplace.

NEW CHALLENGES FOR EXECUTIVE EDUCATION

New standards, new strategies, and new cultures are not easy to come by. Well-managed companies are enlisting every function in the push to become more competitive. Consequently, executive education has also come under closer scrutiny. The CEO is asking how executive education can help shape the culture, communicate and implement the new strategies, and increase productivity in order to become more competitive.

Figure 1-1. Conclusions of EDA 1988 Executive
Development Survey.

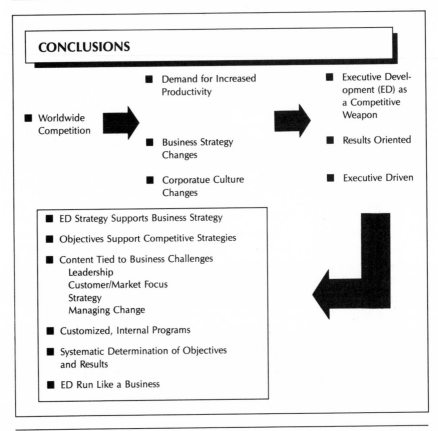

©1988 by Executive Development Associates

How can executive education help senior management in some very
specific and tangible ways? In many a blue-chip company—as we shall
see in this book—the executive education function has responded to
that question with programs that have three common denominators:

- Executive education is given a mission and a set of objectives that
  position it as a competitive weapon.
- Rather than being "general education," programs are results-oriented;
  they are designed and implemented to help participants improve
  the competitiveness and profitability of their corporations.

- Since executive education is directly linked to strategy, the programs are typically supported by top management, often by the chief executive officer.

This new orientation has lead to several fundamental changes in the executive development function itself.

1. Executive education in many companies now has—usually for the first time—a clearly articulated (written) mission that is directly linked to the corporate business strategy. By contrast, executive education often operated in the past in a vacuum and as a "sidecar" to the main business.
2. Executive education programs now have specific objectives that are seen as valuable adjuncts to a company's fight to remain competitive in the global marketplace.
3. The content of the programs is tailored to the unique challenges and opportunities of individual corporations. High-priority subjects include leadership, becoming customer/market-driven, formulating and implementing strategy, and engineering and managing change.
4. Executive education programs are based on the needs of the individual organization and customized to address those requirements. This is essential if the programs are to truly support an organization's unique competitive challenges.
5. There is a more systematic determination of objectives and results. Objectives of executive education programs are developed from thorough needs assessments, which often take the form of in-depth interviews with senior executives to determine what they see as the major changes, challenges, and development needs facing the organization.
6. The executive development function is run like a business and is professionally managed and staffed. Its leaders are at ease in corporate boardrooms and are valued members of the senior team. It is held accountable for results.

What we would now like to do is get behind these conclusions and look at our 1988 survey findings in more detail.

Influences On Executive Development

Participants were asked to indicate the extent to which environmental, social, and business conditions have influenced and will continue to influence executive education. As Figure 1–2 indicates, seven fctors will have anywhere from a moderate to a large impact on the shape and focus of executive development.

The top three conditions influencing executive development for the next three to five years—increased competition, changing business strategies, and the need for greater productivity—are the same as the top three cited in the past. Only their order has shifted somewhat, with respondents answering that "increased competition" was their third-place concern in the past but would be in first place in the future.

Two other factors are also showing significantly greater influence. "Global competition," which, of course, is closely linked to competition

Figure 1–2. Average Ratings of the Extent to Which Conditions Influence Executive Development.

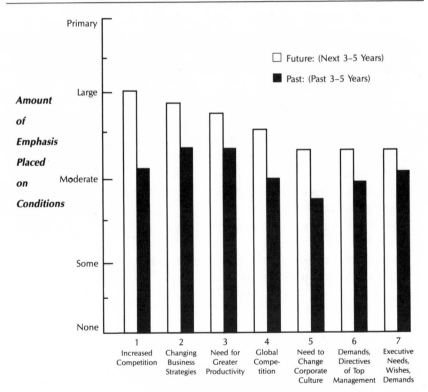

Conditions Influencing Executive Development

generally, moved from fifth place to fourth place, and "the need to strengthen or modify corporate culture" moved from seventh place to fifth place.

One participant observed that "both domestic and global competition are emerging as the dominant influence shaping executive education. We've seen industry after industry—from cars to computers—subjected to more and more competition. Corporate leaders have gotten the message. To stay on top, you must continue to improve and constantly hone your executive talents and expose them to new ideas and new concepts. To stand still in today's global marketplace is actually to lose ground."

Topics for Executive Education

Survey participants were asked to indicate the amount of attention their companies gave to certain topics in the past, as well as the amount of attention they would likely receive in the future. The highlights are depicted in Figure 1–3.

Two particularly significant findings are worth elaborating on. First, the amount of attention that "leadership" is likely to receive in the next

Figure 1–3. Average Ratings of Emphasis Placed on Different Topics for Executive Education.

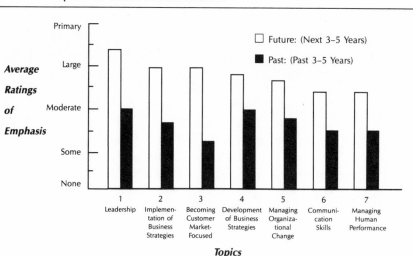

three to five years is nearly double what it was in the past three to five years. "There is a growing acceptance of the idea," wrote a survey participant, "that leadership not only can be taught, but that it should be at the core of any good executive education curriculum. In today's world, we simply cannot survive without strong, competent executive leadership. It's fundamental to our continued success."

Second, the topics ranked in second, third, and fourth place of importance for the years immediately ahead are all hard-nosed business subjects: "implementation of business strategies," "becoming customer/market-focused," and "development of business strategies." The first two topics were virtually unheard of in executive development circles a decade ago.

One participant made a particularly salient observation: "The key challenge for executive development is preparing people and organizations for increasing change and competition. The focus needs to move from standard practices, such as controlling and delegating, to vision, leadership, and implementing business strategies."

Objectives of Executive Education Programs

Not surprisingly, the objectives of executive education programs are also forecasted to be linked more directly to day-to-day business concerns, as Figure 1–4 illustrates. In fact, "addressing key business issues" leads the list of objectives, closely followed by "developing a general management perspective." In addition to this latter objective, "developing a shared vision and unity of purpose" and "shaping and managing culture" also gained in importance.

Survey participants commented eagerly not only about the past and future objectives of executive development, but also about the discipline attached to developing them. Said one: "The rules in this respect are really changing. When I started out in this function, we had some very fuzzy objectives that were never clearly defined and articulated. No more. Now I'm required to specify exactly what a particular module of a particular program is intended to accomplish. There are no more freebies. It's more rigorous and, frankly, more stimulating."

This sentiment was echoed by a number of people who wrote comments about the need for "objectives that can be measured" and "objectives that relate specifically and directly to the corporate mission

Figure 1-4. Average Ratings of the Importance of Executive Education Program Objectives.

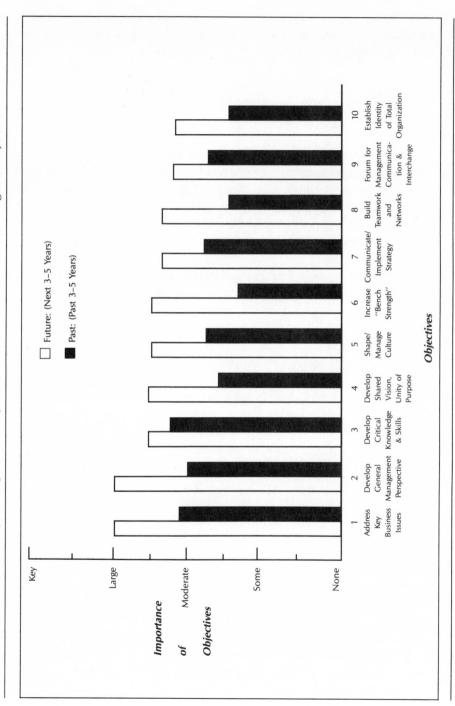

statement." This is a far cry from the days when executive education programs were seen as "nice to do" for a few individuals, but as not terribly effective or relevant for the organization.

Sources and Amounts of Executive Development

Survey participants were asked to identify the amount and source of education and training that their executives and managers had received and would receive in the next three to five years. For the purposes of the survey, three target groups were looked at: very senior executives (including CEOs, presidents, and COOs), all other executives, and high-potential managers. We'll look briefly at each group.

Senior Executives.   On average, CEOs, presidents, and COOs will spend just under one week in executive education programs annually. This is virtually unchanged from the past three to five years. But the *type* of program they will attend is noteworthy. Executives at this level are expected to spend virtually no time on off-the-shelf programs, and very little time on programs developed by internal staff or on external seminars.

On the other hand, there is a decided increase in the number of these very senior executives who will attend a customized in-company program designed for their corporation by outside consultants. Twenty-four percent of the participants estimated that executives will spend one to two weeks in these kinds of programs in the next three to five years.

Other Executives.   There is a significant increase in the amount of time that "all other executives" will spend in development activities—from one week or less in the past three to five years to between one and two weeks in the next three to five years. Survey participants estimated that these executives will devote the most time in the future to programs conducted at universities and to customized programs developed by consultants.

High-Potential Managers.   Not surprisingly, participants estimate that high-potential managers will devote the largest amount of time to education programs in the next three to five years. Customized programs developed by consultants and programs conducted at universities show the greatest increase in the estimated amount of time that will be devoted to them as compared with the amount of time that was devoted to them in the past three to five years—from an average of less than one week to an average of one to two weeks.

Activities of the Executive Development Function

Our study also attempted to assess the types of activities that executive development functions are engaged in and how they are likely to change in the immediate future.

Policies and Strategies.   The survey indicates that the executive development function is becoming increasingly formalized about policies and strategies. Most companies reported, for example, that they had developed a formal written policy on executive education and that a core corporate curriculum had been developed.

On the age-old question of whether it is better to have a centralized executive development function at the corporate level or a decentralized function at the division or business unit level, the scales tipped slightly—but only slightly—toward a centralized function. Yet there does seem to be some impetus toward even more centralization. Thirty-five percent of the survey participants indicated that their centralized staff was likely to increase over the next three to five years. Only 12 percent indicated that their decentralized staff was likely to increase.

Two activities were seen as taking on more importance in the years ahead. The first is increased emphasis on developing and implementing ways to measure changes in the knowledge and skills of executives as a result of executive development activities. Says one participant:

> Increasingly, it won't be good enough just to put on a course and have the students evaluate it. That's a bit of a cop-out because they respond in part to whether or not they *like* the course and whether or not they *thought* they got something out of it. That won't cut it in the future. I'm already being asked to develop ways to measure how people change and grow as a result of executive development *and* how that growth impacts the bottom line. Why not? We measure everything that's important in business. And executive development is now seen as important.

The second cluster of activities that will take on greater importance centers around formalization of the executive development function.

We are likely, for example, to see a trend toward written corporate policies on executive development and the creation of core curriculums. "As we get taken more seriously," says one survey respondent, "we undoubtedly will become more formalized and institutionalized. I don't think that this is a sign of bureacracy, but rather a sign that we have arrived."

Planning and Needs Analysis.   Two activities in this area are growing in importance:

- Suggestions and requests from top managers, who are becoming more vocal and more knowledgeable about their own needs
- Surveys or interviews with prospective program participants as a means of eliciting from them what they want and, just as importantly, what they don't want out of executive development

In our experience, those programs work best in which the participants have been consulted and listened to first. The survey findings provide ample evidence that this is becoming more and more the norm.

Another emerging trend along these lines is the use of subordinates in helping to determine the developmental needs or their bosses. After all, they are the "customer" when it comes to their bosses' leadership and management practices. Some companies survey a cross-section of employees to see what they feel their managers need in the way of development.

Still another vehicle that is gaining momentum and is likely to take on more importance in the next three to five years is membership in consortia with other companies. "Attendance at these meetings," wrote one participant, "is one of the very best uses of my time. I get to share experiences, to learn from the successes *and* failures of others, and to keep abreast of some real leading-edge thinking."

Program Design and Development.   The survey found that the use of systematic evaluation procedures to measure and improve course effectiveness is estimated to increase dramatically in importance over the next three to five years. In addition, formal or informal training to upgrade the design and development skills of internal training staffs is expected to be emphasized more in the next three to five years.

A number of companies expect to increase their emphasis on research on new program design and learning methods. Sixty-three percent of participants indicated that this activity will receive at least moderate

Figure 1–5.   Average Ratings of Emphasis Placed on Different Learning Methods.

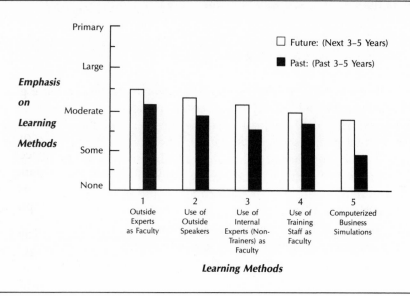

emphasis in the next three to five years, as compared with 46 percent for the previous three to five years.

Learning Methods.   Participants were asked to rank a list of methods that are being used and will be used in executive development. The top five are shown in Figure 1–5. The only newcomer to the list was "computerized business simulations." Respondents indicated that its degree of importance would double in the next three to five years, as compared with the past three to five years. This learning method is relatively new in executive development and is described in some detail in Chapter 2. Other learning methods that were not listed in the top five but are increasing in popularity included satellite programs, computer technology (such as interactive video), and outdoor experiences.

OTHER RESEARCH

Our findings may well be the most specific in the field of executive development. Yet we are not alone. The trends we identified are corroborated by a number of other studies by respected researchers. We have chosen to report here the results of two such studies, in large part because of their timeliness; each was published in early 1988.

Carlisle-Carter Study

A. Elliot Carlisle, professor of management at the University of Massachusetts, and Kent Carter, assistant professor of management at the University of Maine, surveyed the presidents of the U.S. Fortune 500 industrial and service companies. The study sought to determine the relative importance of eight corporate objectives: profitability, financial condition of the firm, productivity, innovation, marketing, management development, worker performance, and public responsibility.

Carlisle and Carter reported their finding in *Business Horizons* (March-April 1988). As Figure 1–6 indicates, the two top-rated items are the financial condition of the firm and profitability. This is hardly surprising. What *is* surprising is that management development ranks third—ahead of such time-honored priorities as marketing and productivity. The researchers concluded that "the firm's survival and growth depends on capable management and orderly succession, and presidents do assign this area a high priority, an indication of concern for the future" (p. 80).

Stephan, Mills, Pace, and Ralphs Study

Another recent study that corroborates our findings was conducted by Eric Stephan, Gordon E. Mills, R. Wayne Pace, and Lenny Ralphs. All four are professors in the Human Resource Program at Brigham Young University. Their research—which also focused on the Fortune 500 companies—was published in *Training and Development Journal* (January 1988).

Several points raised by their research results are especially noteworthy:

- Of 228 topics for executive education, "leadership, including problem-solving, decision-making and competitiveness" was the topic most frequently mentioned by respondents as one they included in their executive education programs.

Those in the executive development function must develop greater access and exposure to senior executives, to corporate strategies, and to objectives and business plans. If they are to fulfill the potential that has opened up to them, they must become full members of the senior management team and must immerse themselves fully in the business. They cannot fulfill their potential if they are operating outside the mainstream as a "nice" but nonessential staff function.

Executive development professionals must be as comfortable in the boardroom as they have been in the classroom, and they must earn the trust and credibility of senior management. Being able to deal effectively with senior executives is critical. But senior executives have never been more open to such collaboration. As one survey participant remarked: "Top management is much more concerned with . . . executive development than it was five years ago. They are putting money, resources, and people behind it and participating themselves. They are also looking to HRD to support company change/competitiveness through executive development more than ever before."

Development professionals must not only acquire business acumen but they must be able to transfer their knowledge of business issues and the direction of the senior executive team into quality products, programs, and processes of executive development that help achieve improvements in the business. They must also be prepared to measure the results of their efforts.

Measuring results is just one aspect of the need among these professionals to focus their efforts more clearly than in the past. Executive development cannot and should not attempt to solve all the issues facing the corporation. But it must understand the key issues, identify the proper role for executive development, gain senior management cooperation, and then strive for results.

The profession has come a long way in the past decade, but we have much more to do. It's an exhilarating time and place to be. This book will tell the story of the enormous impact that executive education is having on some of America's premier companies.

2 HOW EXECUTIVES LEARN: NEW CHALLENGES— NEW METHODS

It will come as no surprise to the reader that the world of executive education is changing at a dramatic pace. Gone are the days when executives were simply sent off to a campus for a week of lectures or shepherded into a classroom to be exposed to a professor's newfound key to motivating the American worker or a consultant's secret weapon for competing with the Japanese.

Writing in *New Management* (Winter 1987), Larry E. Greiner, professor of management and organization at the University of Southern California, points out that much of executive education in the past decade has been in the "entertainment mode."

"My experience," he says, "and I have compared notes with several business school professors and corporate human resources executives, suggests that 'entertainment without development' accounts for about 75 percent of the management education budget (p. 37)."

He goes on to point out that this large—and largely wasted—expenditure includes "all of the glitzy off-the-shelf programs being sold to companies by training and counsulting firms and the current celebrity series fad, in which celebrity speakers, at $10,000 a speech, drop into the executive suite for a couple of hours to talk to celebrity executives who are guided by a celebrity moderator (p. 38)."

Greiner makes a good point. Yet, as he himself indicates, things have begun to change in the executive classroom. In fact, a good deal of executive education no longer even takes place in the classroom. Although case studies and guest speakers are still important and still valuable, the trend is decidedly towards new methodologies for the delivery of executive education.

A common element in the new methods of executive education is the use of experiential learning. Today's executive is as likely to spend a part of his or her executive education experience sitting around a camp fire on the Colorado River as in a classroom at Harvard, Stanford, or Columbia. This chapter explores just a few of the many new methodologies that are being used to help executive education meet the challenges of today's business world. Specifically, we'll look at how outdoor learning, feedback, customer involvement, and business simulations are being used in executive education.

OUTDOOR EXPERIENCES

Until recently, no one would have believed that top executives would be caught dead attending an outdoor program. Yet the outdoor experience is now at the top of virtually everyone's list of successful executive education methods. Although this method has been around for a long time, its popularity has soared in recent years, and it has achieved almost "fad" status. As with all new fads, it has its share of detractors as well as fanatical supporters. The key to success, as with any other technique of executive development, is *first* determining what it is you want to accomplish, and *then* deciding if an outdoor experience can help you.

Although there are dozens of outdoor learning programs on the market, most of them can be grouped into two general categories. The first focuses on challenging and pushing the participant both mentally and physically, often beyond his or her limits, with the secondary purpose of teaching teamwork and leadership. Participants are encouraged to take risks, to overcome fear, and to assume personal challenges that stretch their capabilities. Teaching vehicles include rappeling, mountain climbing, rafting, and surviving in the wilderness.

The second category of outdoor experience focuses on the development of leadership and teamwork and uses the outdoors merely as the environment in which this learning takes place. These programs do not push people to their limits. Rather, the message is that tasks often need teams to accomplish them, and teams usually need leaders. The physical challenges are designed to be well within the limits of all participants.

"When it works," says Patricia Galagan, editor of *Training and Development Journal,* "adventure-based, experiential learning makes you feel like you are 'between two trapezes.' This is the phrase to describe the state between letting go of one stage and starting another. Most change theorists agree that one must travel through this turbulent, un-chartered zone before any real, intentional change can occur (p. 40)."

Galagan notes that the benefit of the outdoor experience is that it takes you far away from your safe and normal habitat and clears the way for you to understand things about yourself that will allow you to change. "The setting for such an experience therefore matters a lot," she says (p. 41).

Another benefit of the outdoor experience is that it cuts down the amount of learning time. It has been well documented that skill in just about anything comes from learning by doing, through a variety of challenging assignments. The outdoor experience represents such assignments, except that consequences are more immediate. In a very short time, many crises occur, providing a powerful means of developing leadership and teamwork.

The goal, therefore, is to place people into situations where they are learning by doing, where there is immediate feedback and where their actions have immediate consequences. The problem for developing leaders in typical situations is that feedback often does not occur for months or years, if at all, thus reducing the opportunity for learning and growth. The objective, therefore, is to provide experience in which this time factor is reduced. Under those conditions, it can be argued that the outdoor experience is one of the best models for rapid, sustained leadership development.

One company that has been particularly aggressive and successful in its use of the outdoor experience is BellSouth. As part of its Management Institute (discussed in Chapter 8), executives are put through a variety of exercises in the outdoors. The objectives, according to BellSouth, are:

- to develop a strong sense of what leadership is and of its importance and role in shaping and guiding BellSouth;
- to understand how to improve personal leadership competency and to acquire the knowledge and commitment to do so; and
- to develop a stronger sense of teamwork, unity of purpose, and esprit de corps.

BellSouth wants its executives to examine leadership in an environment where the consequences are immediate, learning time is reduced, the situations are real, and the experiences are different, interesting, and exciting.

The experiences that the BellSouth executives go through certainly meet that bill. In one, the "leader" is asked to locate and move barrels of toxic material before they explode and contaminate a river. To have any chance of success, the leader must break the group into two teams— one at the top of the cliff, the other at the bottom. If the leader also listens for suggestions, allocates time and people well, plans before acting, maintains good communication, gives clear directions, acts decisively, keeps out of his or her people's way, and is concerned about safety, the operation can be performed with relative ease. In other words, if the leader leads, the task can be completed.

An observer to one such group observed,

> You are immediately reminded that in any given group, you generally have the expertise you need to get the task accomplished. Putting people into a challenging outdoor situation makes the risks obvious and the consequences immediate. Using the outdoors as a classroom is a novelty and a powerful one. It throws people off balance, but it gives them an understanding they can take back to their jobs.

This methodology is not without its detractors. Some people point to accidents, even deaths, that have taken place when inexperienced and unfit executives go into the wilderness. Others point to the psychological damage that can result when an individual is pushed too far and forced to quit or even break down in front of his or her peers. Obviously, the more strenuous the outdoor activities, the higher the likelihood of such problems. The only answer to these and other objections is: use good judgment and common sense. As in many other fields, there are consultants of all levels of competence. In our experience, choosing the right firm is critical.

This warning notwithstanding, the evidence is mounting that outdoor experiences work well with executives. Writing in *Training and Development Journal* (March 1987), Janet Lang gives this particularly vivid description of the impact that the outdoor experience can have when people return to work:

> Tension pulsed through the conference room. Nine district managers grappled with a decreasing market share. The "problem-solving" session had deteriorated into accusations, posturing, and a scramble for declining

resources. The competitive spirit that kept this corporation alive in a volatile marketplace was undermining its management process with cancerous efficiency.

A frustrated pause in the discussions: nine adept mental masons were busy erecting walls when a year-old image diverted one. An intense, no-nonsense corporate veteran of 55 broke the silence: "Gentlemen, this is *not* the way we did it in the woods." Eight startled pairs of eyes met his. Brows softened . . . a smile or two . . . a couple of wistful nods. They could have referred to the list of standards for team interaction they had drawn up in the woods, but they didn't need to. Each was visiting his own durable image—of boosting each other over a 13-foot wall, cheering one another past the mental dragons on the high ropes course, laughing together over their awkwardness and "process blunders" as they solved such weighty problems as crossing an imaginary alligator-ridden swamp with seemingly inadequate resources.

They had talked openly about the very real swamps back in the workplace, and now, hip deep in one, they called on an intellectual memory and a kinesthetic imprint of success in getting the team through intact. The discussion that followed was considerably more solution-oriented (pp. 30–31).

The value of these outdoor experiences rests on a very simple premise: "What I hear, I forget; what I see, I know; what I do, I understand." Thus, when one goes to hear a speech, it is quickly forgotten. If the speaker uses audiovisuals, learning is enhanced. But the individual who *gives* the speech gains the greatest understanding of the subject matter. By the same token, the person who leads—particularly in the life-and-death, totally different environment of the outdoors—gains a keen understanding of leadership.

FEEDBACK

Another popular method of executive education is receiving feedback about your own management style and behavior. Not too long ago, the idea of executives being willing to tolerate, much less appreciate, feedback from subordinates and peers on their effectiveness was farfetched. Increasingly, however, large corporations are concerned not only with the results their executives achieve but with the values, management style, and leadership skills they need to achieve them.

David T. Kearns, chairman and chief executive officer of Xerox Corporation, is fond of pointing out that he wants to lead "not just a big company, but a great company; not just an efficient company, but a values-oriented company." He is not alone. In our experience, virtually every large corporation has expended a great deal of time and effort on agreeing to and articulating a set of corporate values. Virtually all of these value statements include references to the primacy of the customer, the criticality of human resources, the commitment to research and development, and the determination to deliver value to the shareholders.

The trick is in taking these well-intentioned but general words and translating them into specific management actions, behaviors, and expectations, and then providing feedback to the individual executive.

One company that has done this particularly well is the Weyerhaeuser Forest Products Company. The "excellent executive," in Weyerhaeuser's view, is one who builds and keeps commitments to the customer, to the company, to being a leader, to the team, and to innovation. But Weyerhaeuser does not stop there. As explained in a company publication, Weyerhaeuser is "committed to identifying and defining the qualities that make executives successful, and helping executives demonstrate these qualities within their own part of the business."

For example, Weyerhaeuser has articulated a set of behaviors to illustrate what this value, "commitment to the customer," means: that is, eight specific acts that serve the customer and build customer importance. Behaviors have been similarly spelled out for each of the other four commitments. All of these behaviors have been incorporated into feedback inventories, which are filled out by each executive's subordinates and peers. Some seventy-four specific behaviors are measured. A sample of behaviors measuring commitment to the customer, for example, includes:

- Consistently treats his/her customers as a top priority.
- Seeks and actively listens to input from his/her customers.
- Searches for a new and better way to meet customer needs.
- Creates a customer and market orientation throughout our organization.

More and more companies are not only using this process but trying it directly to executive education experiences. This feedback process normally includes:

- Sending the feedback instrument to subordinates and peers of the executive approximately four to six weeks before an executive education program
- Also having the executive complete the instrument so that self-perceptions can be compared to those of subordinates and peers

- Returning the feedback instruments to an outside third party to assure both the respondents and the executive that the feedback is anonymous and confidential
- Tabulating and analyzing the data and generating an individualized written report for each executive
- Having a faculty "coach" present the report to the executive in a one-to-one session during the executive education program to help interpret the messages and consider what could be done to improve
- Developing an action plan for self-improvement and for building on strengths and modifying or coping with weaknesses
- Sharing the key messages received with the team back on the job to ensure understanding and clarify what will be done to improve leadership and teamwork

It should be emphasized that the emphasis of good feedback mechanisms is *not* on the gathering of data, but rather on using that data as a diagnostic tool for self-improvement. A case in point is BellSouth, where executives are told: "There are only two things that we need to do to improve ourselves and reach our full potential: (1) make sure that we obtain comprehensive, objective, and accurate information about our capabilities; (2) develop high-impact plans that we actually *implement*."

This emphasis on implementation at BellSouth and elsewhere is in keeping with the general trend in executive education toward becoming more results-oriented. Scanning the comments from feedback participants, one is struck by the constant references to action and implementation. Typical comments from one recent feedback experience included:

Most powerful event in career so far—will definitely change the way I manage and perform back on the job.

For the first time in my career, I received useful, developmental feedback in a manner that I could immediately put to use on the job.

Learning new techniques to improve yourself can, and in my case will, facilitate definite action.

Of course, this type of feedback can also be used outside of a structured executive development program. One of the first major corporations to use feedback in this way was Xerox Corporation. The feedback system now in place there has evolved slowly, but steadily, over a period of two decades. "That evolutionary process," says one Xerox executive, "is well worth copying. For many managers, feedback is threatening, so you have to introduce it gradually. It should also evolve to meet the changing needs of the organization."

"We've been doing that for so long," says one Xerox manager, "that it's no longer threatening. It's part of our culture and accepted by managers as a normal part of their management process and responsibility."

As the process became institutionalized, it was also adapted to various parts of the organization. One particularly instructive example was in Xerox's Reprographics Business Groups (RBG). In 1981, Xerox reorganized into more decentralized business units in order to become more competitive against the Japanese. Writing in *Management Review* (March 1986), Norman Deets, manager of human resources management in RBG, and Dr. Richard Morano, the RBG manager of organization effectiveness and technical education, described the situation this way:

> A key part of the strategy was to increase the acceptance and commitment of a high-tech work force to a large number of changes occurring at a rapidly increasing rate. This included an increased emphasis on innovation and risk taking. It also meant developing an environment that encouraged a greater work force participation. To accomplish this RBG would have to change the way it managed technical and manufacturing employees. It wanted more openness and trust, needed to encourage more questioning and invite new ideas—a dramatic change for some managers who had grown up under a different system" (p. 31).

Moving to this management style was no easy task. After nearly two years of soul-searching, pilots, and testing, managers developed for themselves a process in which their employees rate them annually, pointing out areas where they are doing well and areas that need improvement.

"Before managers can change the way they manage," write Deets and Morano, "they have to know what changes are needed in their current style. They also should know what aspects of their style are considered strengths and should not be changed. The starting point for improving management style, therefore, is an honest assessment of the manager's current behavior by his or her workers" (p. 33).

To that end, managers ask their employees to complete a 44-item questionnaire that covers such behaviors as task management, communications, people development, employee involvement, and leadership. Results from this process are impressive. When the RBG feedback mechanism was evaluated, it was found that:

- 78 percent of managers regularly discussed effective management behavior with their subordinates;
- 83 percent created action plans for their own self-improvement;
- 84 percent of these not only started but continued with their action plans;
- 85 percent express confidence that their own styles will improve by the following year; and
- 66 percent feel that the feedback survey is an important tool to help them improve.

The last time the feedback process was fully evaluated, the program's results were gratifying. The percentage of managers receiving positive ratings ("adequate" to "extremely good") increased from 72.7 percent to 82 percent. During the same period the percentage of managers receiving negative ratings ("poor" to "adequate") decreased from 27.3 percent to 17.8 percent.

These are impressive results. Perhaps that's why Xerox is hardly alone. As the reader will see in this book, a number of leading corporations are using feedback as a potent aid in getting executives to identify their strengths and weaknesses, to develop action plans for improvement, and to then evaluate how they are doing.

CUSTOMER INVOLVEMENT

Still another methodology becoming more widely used in in-company executive education programs is customer involvement. It's no wonder. Much of American industry has been forced to relearn a very painful lesson in recent years: the customer, and the customer alone, ultimately determines the success or failure of any business enterprise. Since the early 1970s, industry after industry has suffered from a failure to focus on the customer. A few examples will illustrate this rather bleak indictment:

- The "Big Three" automotive companies—General Motors, Ford, and Chrysler—continued to give us big gas-guzzlers that looked good when we wanted economical cars that ran well.
- The U.S. electronics industry continued to give us choices and options at a premium price when what we wanted was standardization at good value.

- The American copier industry continued to give us features and options at high prices when what we wanted was quality and good value.

For a time, American industry got away with turning its back on what the customers wanted. That was because consumers by and large had few options. In most industries, it was "buy American" or don't buy at all. What competition existed in many industries was weak and fragmented.

All that changed dramatically in the 1970s for two very different reasons. First, foreign competition, long a slumbering giant, suddenly awakened and began its relentless attack on the American market at the expense of American corporations. And second, the Reagan administration led a thrust toward deregulation—which introduced several industries that had once been protected to the harsh realities of a competitive marketplace.

Many American business leaders have woken up to this new reality. Charles W. Moritz, chairman and chief executive officer of Dun and Bradstreet, put it this way: "The vendor who fails to provide customer value is going to lose that customer to a competitor who does—a vendor who has listened better, heard better, and has the courage to act even when such action necessitated change."

In *In Search of Excellence,* the best-selling book of the mid-1980s, Thomas J. Peters and Robert H. Waterman, Jr., cite the work of Citibank's Dinah Nemeroff. She examined a group of companies known for their customer focus and found that two common denominators made them different—intensive, active involvement on the part of senior management and a high degree of feedback, exhibited by a willingness to listen to the customer.

Combining these two principles—senior management involvement and customer feedback—has become a key element in executive development programs for several of America's leading corporations. This handful of corporations includes AT&T, Xerox, Northern Telecom, and Weyerhaeuser. Here's a brief look at how executive education works at each one of them.

AT&T

AT&T, faced with the need to become more customer focused in the aftermath of deregulation, involves customers in a half-day discussion as part of a five-week executive development seminar. Two or three key managers from a major customer are invited. AT&T makes its intentions quite clear. The letter of invitation states: "Let me stress that this is not a sales meeting. Rather, we need your help in gaining a better understanding of the needs of our customers; what you see as our major strengths and weaknesses; and your recommendations for how AT&T can improve customer relations with clients in general and you in particular." The letter urges customer representatives "to be as candid and critical as you like. Our objective is to see ourselves as the customer sees us." After a two-hour discussion with the customer, the AT&T executives split up into small groups to identify specific actions they can take back on the job to improve customer satisfaction.

Xerox

Though not a victim of deregulation, Xerox did fall prey to foreign competition—particularly from the Japanese. Its market share deteriorated from near-monopoly proportions in the early 1970s to less than a 50 percent share by the end of the decade. CEO David T. Kearns instituted the Xerox Senior Management Program—a week-long executive development program that his top 250 executives attended over the course of a year. Central to the seminar was a section on customer satisfaction, a major plank in Kearns's strategy.

Senior representatives of major Xerox customers—such as Westinghouse, Digital Equipment Corporation, and Manufacturers Hanover Trust—were invited to give presentations on what they did and did not like about Xerox, with the emphasis on the latter.

Put on the firing line, the senior executives of Xerox heard criticism from customers in an environment conducive to openness. For some executives, it was the first time they had ever had face-to-face feedback from customers. For virtually all, it was the first opportunity to meet in a nonselling situation and get candid opinions.

Said one Xerox executive who went through the experience: "It hurts to hear that you're far from perfect. You want to be defensive, but then you realize it's tough medicine that's for your own good. You can't continue to be a leader without the knowledge of what's wrong and what needs to be fixed."

Northern Telecom

The approach that Northern Telecom (NTI) takes is very similar, with one important twist.

The telecommunications giant prides itself on its technological leadership. It was feared that executives would be too busy defending the status quo to really listen to the criticism of customers. So the marketing vice president of NTI introduced the customer panel by defusing that issue. He emphasized that "whether or not we succeed depends almost entirely on the customer's *perception* of NTI. What we think of our customer service is of little consequence. What really matters is what the *customer* thinks."

After the customer presentations, NTI executives break up into small groups to decide and plan actions that they personally can take to improve customer satisfaction. Says one: "We are not doing this for fun. We're doing it to take what we've learned and translate it into specific actions to improve the quality of our customer service. These are powerful, compelling messages, and we must act quickly and decisively in response."

Weyerhaeuser Forest Products Company

The Weyerhaeuser Forest Products Company (FPC) invites its customers to attend for four full days in its week-long program entitled "Creating and Leading a Customer/Market-Driven Enterprise." That's right—*four days*! They join the FPC executives as learning partners who immediately apply the program concepts to their business relationship.

FPC means business. One person who is familiar with the program and, in fact, was involved in its design, describes its intent in rather blunt terms:

> To be honest with you, a lot of our senior people were out of touch with the customer. The focus was on whatever is good for Weyerhaeuser is good for the customer. We wanted to bring them face to face with customers who were a little angry and feeling a lot neglected. We also wanted to get across the concept that the company and the customers were in partnership with one another. That's precisely what happened.

Executives and customers work together to identify the type of market orientation that FPC needs so that *both* the company and its customers can be successful. By creating an atmosphere of partnership, the focus is not only on the customer but on identifying opportunities that neither could identify alone. Executives and managers from all segments of the Weyerhaeuser business attend these programs because, in the words of Charley Bingham, CEO of FPC: "Only after a customer is in view can we worry about our human, capital, and raw material resources. There is no other reason to have a business or a staff department to provide a product called 'accounting' . . . or an operating unit . . . producing lumber."

Lynn Endicott, vice president of Weyerhaeuser's Building Products Group, describes the experience this way: "We're directing all the energy of our company toward the marketplace and the customer. This program is the catalyst—the way we intend to harness that energy and cause things to happen that we never thought possible before."

And how do the customers view the opportunity to "level" with one of their major suppliers? Al Newkirk, chairman of Chandler Lumber Company, a major supplier to the southern California building industry, says, "Unbelievable. I've never seen such a commitment toward understanding my needs and my customers' needs before. It gives me a good feeling about American business."

Thorry Gunnersen, managing director of the Australian Marbut Gunnersen Group, thinks customers learn as much FPC management. "I'm going home better able to run my own company, and that's beyond any expectations I had for the program," he commented.

The programs at AT&T, Xerox, Northern Telecom, and Weyerhaeuser are hardly panaceas. But they are important pieces of the solution. As such, they offer excellent examples of how executive development is seeking new and creative ways to apply itself to the real work problems of the corporation.

In "How to Get People to Do Things," Robert Conklin tells the story of a 14-year-old boy was telling his mother about his girlfriend. The mother asked why he thought his girlfriend was so fond of him. "She likes me because she thinks I'm handsome, fun, smart, and dance good," the boy replied.

"And how about you? Why do you like her so much?" the mother asked.

"Because she thinks I'm handsome, fun, smart, and dance good," the boy replied.

There's a bit of that feeling in all of us. We are drawn toward people who make us feel important. And that's as true in the world of big business as it is in teenage romance. Says William O. McCoy, president of BellSouth Enterprises, "Customers gravitate to companies that make it clear they want to satisfy and please just as much as they want to close a sale. To establish that feeling with a customer, and build it into a long-standing relationship, sets the great companies apart from those that never quite rise to excellence."

BUSINESS SIMULATIONS

Another executive education methodology that is drawing increased attention and application is the use of business simulations. This type of executive development is, of course, a natural response to the increasing demand for more hands-on and results-oriented developmental experiences.

In "Games People Play" (*Sky,* May 1985), Bernie Ward observes that terms like *games* and *play* may seem like "misnomers when applied to the solemn mien of the corporate boardroom. But just as children learn through playing, thousands of executives today are playing real-life management games intended to modify behaviors, provide insights, and thus improve their craft as individuals and the fortunes of their companies. These games all operate on a single premise: You learn best by doing" (p. 72).

Good management, the theory goes, is not an inherent skill. You may be able to learn the concepts in a classroom setting, but you have not really learned them until you have put them into use. The emergence of business simulations is one concrete way to help managers do this.

One of the first simulations recreates a business world in which the players are exposed to the equivalent of four years of executive experience. The game is typically played by six people who sit around a traditional game board. Each player has "risk" and "decision" cards and chips that represent resources: workers, raw materials, machines, research and development, finished products, advertising, and so on. Forms are also provided that enable each player to chart cash flows, close accounts, and develop strategic plans.

Each player starts with $30,000 of venture capital, forms a company, competes with other game players, and is responsible for every aspect of business operation. Each "year," as "president," each player develops a strategic plan, invests in resources such as quality control and advertising, sets up purchasing, production and distribution facilities, hires personnel, manages cash flows, analyzes expenses, and prepares financial statements. To add a little drama, the simulation also introduces an element of real-world risk—fire in an uninsured warehouse, for example, or the unexpected loss of a key executive.

Business simulations are almost universally well received. One participant finds business simulation to be "much superior to lecture-type seminars" and "the best way I know to experience how all the various functions in the corporation are interrelated." Another observed: "The experience was much more detailed and complicated than I had originally thought. It is three days well spent and gives me a better insight into planning for more profitable results. It's the best management development experience I've ever had."

One participant experienced a real breakthrough: "In my seven years in the retail business, I have usually tuned out in-depth conversations regarding financial figures. One reason is that no one had explained certain procedures in a way I could understand them. Now I am confident I will be able to participate more. I am no longer intimidated by accounting procedures!"

Another popular simulation puts a group of senior managers into the top twenty executive positions, ranging from chief financial officer to vice president of sales, in a fictitious company. Each manager receives a wealth of background information on the company—everything from a balance sheet to a marketing study—and individualized in-baskets chockful of mail, memos, problems, and challenges. They are then turned loose to manage the company for a day. The day's pace, issues, and challenges are typically so like their real-world equivalents that the participants quickly get into the simulation and begin to behave and manage much like they do back on the job.

This is key to the success of this type of program. An important element of the program is the "debriefing" that takes place after the simulation. The debriefing gives managers a chance to do what they seldom can do in their real jobs: reflect on what they did and analyze its implications for their management style and behavior. Participants hear firsthand from instructors, as well as from the other participants, how well they made decisions, delegated assignments, shared information with subordinates and peers, solved problems, and handled conflicts.

The purpose of debriefings is gaining self-awareness. How did the organization function? How did the participant function and perform as part of the organization? How were problems resolved? How were decisions made? The approach is inductive: managers start by examining their own behavior in the simultation and then go on to extract lessons about management that apply specifically to themselves back on the job.

In "Games That Teach You to Manage" (*Fortune*, 29 October 1984), Peter Petre's description of the experience of one manager with this type of business simulation provides useful insights:

> When William Clabby agreed to participate in a management-training exercise . . . last year, he didn't expect to learn much he didn't already know. A vice president at Dow Jones, Clabby, 53, thought he already understood how to get results. He was known around the publishing company as a hard charger and an intimidating boss who challenged the details of subordinates' work and disciplined lazy staffers by timing their lunch hours. . . .
>
> Bill Clabby and some of his colleagues would get a chance to show their managerial stuff by running for one day a make-believe glass manufacturing company with 4,000 employees and $200 million in annual sales.
>
> When the players reported for work at 9 the next morning, they were shown to desks with telephones and full in-boxes. Clabby's in-box held more than 50 memos, whose subject matter ranged from the important to the inconsequential . . . [the company] had a chance to make a big acquisition; the advance products division was torn over where to locate a new plant; the division that made windshields couldn't keep up with demand. Clabby began to manage. Scanning memos furiously, he grabbed the phone, inviting his vice presidents for a 9:15 meeting. While waiting for them, he quickly decided that the papers provided him lacked the financial data he needed. Clabby punched the phone again, and this time got a member of the training staff. "Does this outfit have a controller?" he asked. "How much money do I have to spend?"
>
> Minutes later Clabby told his vice presidents that, besides solving the problems in the in-boxes, one of their goals would be to invest $45 million by the day's end. He instructed them to report back to him every hour on the hour and sent them back to work. It was 9:22.
>
> By the end of the day, Clabby's group had lit up the scoreboard, correctly identifying and solving over half the 99 problems buried in the in-boxes (no one ever solves them all). . . . [the company's] return on equity, tabulated when the flurry of activity was over, had leaped to 12.6%.
>
> Clabby was triumphant when he learned of his success the next day, which was devoted to "debriefing" the participants. In the course of the debriefing, though, he began to wonder if he hadn't missed the point of the exercise. To his amazement, three vice presidents politely accused him of cutting them out of decisions. They also suggested that he had seemed unaware of the complexity of the problems they faced and offered too little guidance about how to solve them.

Co-workers say Clabby came back . . . a changed man—mellower, more solicitous of employees' views, and slower to explode when handed bad work. "People say I learned," he admits. "You can look in the mirror, but you don't see yourself. People have to say how you look."

Some business simulation games are extremely complex. For example, in yet another, participants are assigned to one of six hypothetical companies that then compete with one another in a complex consumer goods industry, such as manufacturing styrofoam cups. The end objective of the exercise is to maximize the stock market capitalization of each firm. The winner, of course, is the one whose company has the highest stock value when the game ends.

When the game starts, each firm is suffering from declining profits, swollen inventories, and insufficient cash. The players can float new stocks, issue bonds, and expand capacities. They also set credit terms, advertising budgets, research and development spending, and dividend policy and make such production decisions as output mix and number of shifts worked. The teams must make these kinds of marketing, production, and financial decisions for their companies each year. Their decisions are fed into a computer model, along with a description of the state of the economy. Each round is evaluated by a computer.

Participants learn that good management is a fine art, requiring a delicate balance. Some companies make drastic cuts in production, employment, and spending and enjoy a dramatic increase in stock price. The success, of course, is short-lived. Other companies boost production, increase advertising expenses, and add to the sales force. Revenues soar, but within a year the company hovers on the brink of bankruptcy.

The executives learn that neither approach is correct. The players who cut costs do so at their own expense. The lack of investment in the future eventually shows up in the unavailability of current products, dissatisfied customers, and no new products in the pipeline. The group that dramatically increases its investment in production and marketing gains short-term revenue but eventually finds it cannot cover the costs of its huge investments. What is required is balance.

An increasing number of blue-chip corporations are jumping on the simulation bandwagon. They include Northern Telecom, Monsanto, Weyerhaeuser, Union Carbide, and AT&T, and the results appear to be uniformly good. Says one expert in the field: "There is cognitive learning involved in lectures and textbooks, but if you're interested in changing how people behave and in creating insights into how they behave, then this kind of simulation has a unique power to do that. I believe that accounts for why they've really taken off."

The discussion in this chapter of some methodologies—outdoor experiences, feedback, customer involvement, and business simulation—is far from exhaustive. These four only begin to illustrate the revolution that is taking place in executive education. The corporate landscape is dotted with other examples—from Socratic seminars to interactive video, from psychodrama to theatre experiences.

The reason for such diversity is, I believe, rather simple. Our corporations are locked in heroic competitive battles—not just for increased market share and improved financial results, but for their very survival. Executive education cannot be part of the problem; it must be part of the solution.

Both chief executive officers and human resource professionals in well-managed companies are recognizing this. In *The Art of Japanese Management* (1981), Richard Pascale and Anthony Athos observe that "top managements, the business schools that train them, and the consultants who advise them have all been faulted for a destructive preoccupation with analytical technique—too narrow in its conception and too short term in its application" (p. 13).

Responding to this criticism, and others like it, senior managers and education professionals have introduced new curricula and new methods for delivering them. Gone are the days when the corporate executive was sent off to the business school for a week-long seminar and then pronounced ready to take on a new assignment or solve an old problem. Business schools will and should always have a critical role in educating our nation's corps of executives, but there is a new realization that these institutions play only a limited role.

It is also becoming clear that as corporations themselves take on more and more of the education of their executives, they will continue to move away from the lecture format to a variety of new and different experiential learning methods in order to engage the interest of executives as well as enhance and accelerate their learning. But as we will see in the next two chapters, some corporations have always been innovative in their executive education efforts.

II MANAGING ORGANIZATIONAL CHANGE

3 GE: 25 YEARS OF TRAINING FOR CHANGE

The General Electric Company is well known throughout the world for its comprehensive and long-term approach to developing executives and senior managers. In fact, *GE-trained* has become a term that is synonymous with excellence in the minds of many.

Every month John ("Jack") Welch, Jr., chairman of the board and chief executive officer of the General Electric Company, goes to GE's Management Development Institute at Crotonville, New York—as both a teacher and a student.

For much of the afternoon and sometimes into the evening he'll wrestle with issues facing the $40 billion organization. Given GE's tradition of "constructive conflict," those attending the institute feel free—perhaps more accurately, obliged—to argue with Welch. When he leaves, the attendees write up formal evaluations of his performance that day; he'll be expected to take that feedback seriously.

CROTONVILLE: TRAINING TO MEET CHALLENGES

Since its beginnings in the 1950s, "Crotonville," as most GE employees call the Management Development Institute, has been unconventional. On the surface, this collegelike complex about an hour from both

Manhattan and GE's headquarters in Fairfield, Connecticut, looks like many other executive conference centers.

The setting is rustic. Attendees stroll around in casual clothes; they don't seem in a hurry. Some ride bikes, others go to the fitness center. Batches of complimentary copies of the *Wall Street Journal* and the *New York Times* keep them in contact with the world outside. The corridors are lined with tables of coffee and soft drinks. But there the similarity to other conference centers ends. No one, including Welch, ever leaves this off-site facility the same person.

Each year, about 60 percent of GE's top people will go to the mat, like Welch, with the participants in the institute's programs. After they leave, heated debates about the issues continue giving off steam long into the night. Nor is the day's work over for the participating executives, who will study the feedback knowing that their performance at Crotonville was as significant as a 10-minute presentation before the board of directors.

Although the debate and confrontation happen spontaneously, the atmosphere of iconoclastic thinking is by design. Crotonville was created in the 1950s by GE's chairman and CEO of the time, Ralph J. Cordiner, to be a catalyst for change.

In fact, back in those days it was viewed as the Fort Dix of GE: a rigorous boot camp that transformed the individual into a genuine member of the GE "family." Every executive was required to serve eighteen weeks at the facility, with no weekends off. At the time, GE wanted to become more decentralized in its structure to bring decisionmaking closer to the contact with the customer. Peter Drucker was one of the many experts who engaged the participants in dialogue about the pros and cons of decentralization. Shrewdly, Cordiner knew that it would take more than a memo to get executives to shift from a highly centralized to a loose, decentralized structure.

When decentralization eventually made the corporate structure grow unwieldy, his successor Frederick Borg would again use executive development to reshape the organization into forty strategic business units. And dealing with the ramifications of double-digit inflation was later one of Reginald Jones's goals when he put a renewed emphasis on executive development.

Over time, GE's Management Development Institute has evolved into what is today a leadership development institute. Its mission is "to enhance GE's competitiveness in a global environment by providing . . . a broad array of experiences while serving as an instrument of cultural change." A company brochure describes Crotonville as "both a comfortable and uncomfortable place." The comfort part is obvious. The discomfort, the brochure points out, begins

> . . . at the doors of the "Pit" and the "Cave" and the other meeting and lecture rooms around the campus. Ideas, opinions, and cherished business beliefs are brought into these rooms by student and faculty alike and are either bought, rethought, or rejected.
>
> Arguments are advanced. Voices are raised. Unsupported opinions [are] dismissed, sometimes gently, sometimes vigorously . . . to help GE become the most competitive enterprise on earth.

The "Pit" is where Welch presents, debates, defends, attacks, and mulls over issues. Like his predecessors—Cordiner, Borg, and Jones—Welch is using executive development as a strategic tool to achieve massive changes in the organization.

These four chairmen's objectives for change have been different, but they share a deep commitment to "executive education as a process to help GE both transform its organization and at the same time maintain what is best about the corporate identity," states James Baughman, Manager, Corporate Management Development.

In that, explains Baughman, GE was a "pioneer." Most industry experts would agree with that claim. Until the early 1980s, the more traditional approach to executive education at many other large corporations consisted of business school–type courses and some training in administration. The focus was on the individual, no link was made between what was learned and the direction or strategy of an organization. Even at GE during times when it was business as usual, observes Baughman, "executive development . . . returned to a more conventional pattern and it was an elective, not required."

Welch assumed his current role in 1981—from then until today business has not been as usual. Those who follow the business media know that Welch has not only responded to change from outside the organization but has made his own changes in the direction of GE's businesses. He has relied heavily on executive development to help the organization assimilate the massive transformations. Learning opportunities at GE extend out from Crotonville to on-site courses and action learning around the globe.

Crotonville is a potent symbol of executive development, but the development process, from the shop floor to the CEO's office, is an ongoing, day-to-day happening at GE. To restrict "development" to those who actually come through Crotonville's doors each year, emphasizes Baughman, "is to miss the whole point of GE's commitment to fostering leadership in all our 350,000 employees."

Starting with Cordiner, GE executives have always seen response to challenges as being the responsibility of the entire GE family. For that reason, the formal executive development program has been linked with human resources training in general. Let's look at four of the critical challenges that Welch has faced or is facing now, and at how he is addressing them by using executive development to link the top management layers with the rest of the organization.

Increasing Global Market Penetration

Like many other U.S. corporations, GE has seen its businesses becoming increasingly global. For example, at one time GE earned much of its revenues from supplying the United States with large power generators and transformers. Over time, however, that market stabilized. To grow, GE had to look offshore. But there the market was already dominated by, among others, the Germans, the Swiss, and the Japanese, all of whom had not only a head start but technical and political advantages as well.

Although GE wasn't the stereotypical American "sleeping giant" that had to be roused from its comfortable slumber, it did have to become leaner and meaner—and more alert. To do that, Welch turned to executive development. He had two major objectives.

The first was attitudinal. "What Welch had to do," explains Baughman, "was get the key people in the organization to think in global rather than regional terms. That meant a new standard of performance. We were now in the global major leagues and we had to reach toward a new standard of excellence."

The second objective concerned business know-how. Here GE has special problems. Like Welch, many of the best and brightest at the company come with a superb technical background. But that has also been something of a liability. Many GE managers not only had gaps in their knowledge of general business, such as accounting or marketing principles and practices, but usually could not even see the need to broaden their expertise. "Many who come to GE," points out Baughman, "like to think that they are joining a type of engineering guild rather than a commercial enterprise."

Business know-how is now transmitted at GE primarily with courses, case studies, and simulations focused on actual GE experiences, problems, and opportunities. That approach differs from more traditional development programs, which do not focus on the specific company or industry and tend to use passive rather than experiential modes of instruction.

In fact, what it calls "action learning" is a central part of development at GE. This action learning approach provides a process for uncovering problems and opportunities, analyzing strategies, and testing ideas. It includes problem-solving as well as implementing fundamental changes for both business teams and organizations. In 1988, for example, executive learning teams, who will compete with one another, are going to Europe to work on actual GE business issues in a variety of settings: the use of plastic applications in the automobile industry, the X-ray market in medical equipment, and leveraged buyouts in financial services.

That trip will provide GE executives with hands-on experience in the complexities of conducting business in the international arena and will also provide European operations with input from GE's best people. All action learning takes place on real projects; actual results are expected.

The "final exam" will take the form of a presentation of findings before the highest ranking official of the host organization. Since at least two different teams will work on the same problem, a competitive element is built into the project. Given the high visibility of the assignment, participants feel the same motivation to succeed that they do in their permanent jobs.

In addition to action projects, most courses are structured to encourage experiential rather than theoretical learning. Rarely is there an instructor who just lectures while students take notes. There are usually opportunities to immediately apply the lessons learned.

For instance, a marketing course, "Exceptional Sales Performance Workshop," uses—and I quote from the course description—"innovative customer-based feedback, small group problem solving, reality testing exercises, individual workbook exercises and cases." In many other marketing courses, customers actually sit in and give their candid appraisals of products and services.

The advanced financial management course divides participants—and again I quote from the course description—into "multi-business teams to encourage the exchange of ideas and to stimulate creative thinking

on the use of financial analysis techniques within and across businesses."
The advanced information technology management course has the same
team structure and the same objective for the use of information
technology. The faculty teaching this course includes both GE executives and university professors in the field of information technology
management, as well as professors from other functional areas such
as marketing, manufacturing, business strategy, and organizational
dynamics.

That diversity of expertise and experience gives students a good sense
of how different functions interrelate. In addition, in most learning situations, including action learning, about 30 percent of the participant
group is from an outside function. That ensures that the participants
get a working knowledge of how, for example, marketing intersects with
finance, or with research and development.

That ability to work across functions has provided GE with competitive advantages, including innovative product development. In "The
Innovators" (*Fortune*, 6 June 1988), Kenneth Labich lists GE as being
among "America's most imaginative companies turning new ideas into
big dollars" (p. 50). What innovative companies have in common,
observes Labich, is "coordination between divisions" (p. 50), and as
an example he cites the teamwork that led to GE's Ultem, a plastic that
could achieve $100 million in sales annually by 1990.

It is interesting and useful to note that in *The General Manager*
(1982), Harvard Business School professor John P. Kotter identifies getting cooperation across functions as one of the six major challenges
facing general managers. When it comes to doing business across functions, executives cannot rely on their authority over those reporting to
them. Throughout their stay at Crotonville, participants are constantly
challenged with the question, "Why should anyone follow you?"

Besides asking questions such as this, GE has discovered another way
of encouraging cooperation across functions. A mix between the generations happens naturally because executive management and development at GE are ongoing processes that take place from the time someone
joins the company until the person retires. In its classrooms, the dining
room, the fitness centers, and the Pit, the generations are exposed to
one another's ways of seeing the business world. Typically, those
worldviews are constantly challenged. If a generational gap exists before
students and faculty come to Crotonville, it has disappeared by the time
they leave. Bridging that gap is central to good working relations, particularly across functions.

Maintaining a Strong Corporate Identity

Welch constantly struggles with maintaining a strong, unifying corporate identity amidst the diversity of the fourteen individual businesses—many of which, such as NBC or Kidder, Peabody Group, Inc., have their own organizational style and traditions. Like his predecessors, Welch does not want GE to be a conglomerate. In analyzing GE's executive leadership in their book *CEO* (1984), Harry Levison and Stuart Rosenthal point out, "When Ralph J. Cordiner, Borg's predecessor, decentralized GE in the early 1950s into 110 businesses, managers were continually reminded they were still part of GE" (p. 20).

GE's brochure on Crotonville explicitly says:

> A key, and prized competitive lever GE possesses that conglomerates do not is that, despite our diversity in businesses, and even cultures, we remain a family, with many shared values and the ability and the desire to help one another compete in an increasingly difficult world.

GE's, and Welch's, emphasis on a unifying corporate identity should not, however, be understood as a desire for a monolithic corporate culture. GE has always prized diversity and has been shrewd enough to see the competitive value of having the individual businesses continue in their own idiosyncratic style and ways of approaching business.

What Welch wants is called "glue" in the world of GE. The company has long believed in the unique synergy of the various businesses joined as a whole. To keep that whole together, there must be the "glue" of a shared value system and standards of excellence. Those values and standards are woven into the fabric of executive education at GE.

The top people from GE's entertainment, financial, aerospace, aircraft, and appliance businesses intermingle in all the Crontonville classes. Directly and indirectly, they learn about the rest of GE and about each other. The most direct way is through analyzing in depth GE's evolving 18-page statement about values.

The amount of intense debate that statement elicits can be surprising—and sometimes the most surprised are the executive participants themselves. Then it dawns on them that they are shaping, and will continually reshape, how 350,000 people conduct themselves in business. In his Pit forums, Welch sets the example: ongoing clarification of professional values and standards of conduct are high-priority matters. The seriousness with which he treats those questions makes it clear to all that the discussions aren't about Ethics 101 but about living business issues.

In addition, since most of the courses cover real-world business problems, the executives get to see both similar and different styles of problem-solving in action. That melting pot of distinct corporate cultures serves to prevent GE as a whole, or any of its business units individually, from becoming insular. Other major companies have to ward off one-dimensionality by importing representatives from other large corporations. GE has built-in diversity—and it taps into it through executive development.

The Management of Downsizing

The third key challenge that Welch must deal with is the simultaneous downsizing of some businesses and the 25 percent growth rate of others. Both require outstanding leadership.

In executive development, the top people at the downsized businesses learn how to approach everything from the criteria for reduction to the need to redesign the actual work load—not just job descriptions—after the reductions. Since the decision to downsize is part of a strategic plan, it should not be surprising that Crontonville is also a key resource in learning how to implement new strategies. For example, executives learn to deal with the increased spans of control that can come with a restructuring.

Perhaps even more difficult for the executives of a downsized business is the adjustment to fewer resources. To thrive despite the additional responsibility on top of more limited resources, executives learn creative ways of reconfiguring the work. Equally important, they must learn to communicate a new spirit to the survivors of the reduction. As both my own work and the recent research of others have pointed out, the continued success of the downsized organization depends on the sensitivity of the leaders.

But excellence in leadership is equally essential to organizations increasing in size and complexity. For instance, executives of rapidly growing businesses must learn that larger does not necessarily mean more of the same. Executives cannot just superimpose what they have already learned about leadership onto the rapidly evolving organization. At Crontonville they find out how to redefine leadership for situations that are substantially different from any they have dealt with before.

All employees at all levels are introduced to the concept of leadership from their first day at GE. When employees move to more demanding leadership roles, it is not without help from GE. Unlike many other companies that believe in "finding" the born leaders in the ranks, GE tends to believe that leaders can be made. Therefore, potential leaders are slowly moved along a continuum—from "leading" just themselves, to leading a small group, to leading larger and more diverse groups, on up to the level of complexity of a CEO's position. At GE, they call the process the "leadership development framework," and it has little to do with job titles per se.

When asked to define leadership, GE employees most frequently respond with the word *vision*. Leadership, to the 350,000 men and women of GE, is the ability to mobilize others to cooperate and achieve the overall mission of being number one or number two in everything they do. Through development and training they learn the skills to catalyze motivation in others—and in themselves.

An important part of that learning, both in courses and on the job, has been continuous feedback. And as the leader of leaders, Welch makes sure that receiving and giving feedback begins with him. As many GE employees will say, "We're not afraid of confrontation, as long as it has a constructive purpose."

The Rapidly Changing Socioeconomic Environment

Welch's fourth major challenge is the rapidly changing world that all corporations must do business in. This environment includes: changes in government regulations, both domestic and international; scientific discoveries that provide new information about the impacts of GE products, such as plastics and nuclear reactors, on health and safety; defense spending policies and priorities; demographics that are reshaping the marketplace; new consumer values; and the evolving profile of tomorrow's workers—for example, by the year 2000 only 20 percent of the American work force will be native-born American males.

Through course work and action projects, executives are called upon to rethink GE's relationship with the worldwide community, particularly with government and opinion leaders, the public, customers, suppliers, and employees. Those relationships are constantly evolving and are fraught with uncertainty. "You won't find the how-to on community relations," stresses Baughman, "in any textbook." That information is derived from GE's actual ongong experience with those key constituencies.

Given the turbulence in the domestic and international marketplaces, GE is prepared to recognize these additional serious challenges and to respond to them through its executive development strategy. In fact, its executive development effort has shifted over the past several years toward a more intense focus on marketing issues. Since Welch is well known for genius and aggressiveness in marketing, the increased attention to reaching customers could reflect his particular stamp on the curriculum. (Borg, for instance, went down in GE history for the COIN (Coping with Inflation) course that was shaped during his tenure.)

EMPLOYEE DEVELOPMENT

Part of GE's success—and the success of its executive and management development—is attributable to its careful sense of timing. First of all, it closely monitors employees at all levels to determine when they are ready to move into another job to enhance their skills. But sometimes it is useful, declares Baughman, "to just leave employees alone to do their jobs."

Secondly, executive and management development are provided when, in GE terminology, employees are "most teachable." Essentially that occurs—and keeps reoccurring—at two watersheds in their careers.

The first is when employees have been in their jobs long enough to have acquired some bruises. After taking enough knocks, they seem ready to pause and reflect on their experience. The second watershed is when employees know that they are ready for a major promotion. Because they are anticipating the challenge ahead, they are eager for new knowledge and intense feedback.

The Core Development Sequence

For this reason, executive and management development has been divided into five distinct phases, which are called the Core Development Sequence. The first two phases are open to new professional hires and managers. The last three are reserved for top executives. Those who make it through all five will be among the top fifty executives in GE. As in Cordiner's days, the Core Development Sequence is required. Given this structure, one might say that executive development is an integral part of the process that makes for a smooth succession within the corporation and its fourteen business units.

Development Stage I.   All new professional hires attend the Corporate Entry Leadership Conference I within six months of their hire date. This conference is held at Crontonville and focuses on company and individual values. Integral to the experience is networking. Participants get to meet their peers and exchange views with general managers and a vice chairman.

During their third year with GE, they attend the Corporate Entry Leadership Conference II. There the focus shifts to the competitive context and the individual employee's role in helping the company achieve its vision.

Development Stage II.   All newly appointed managers attend the New Manager Development Program. There they concentrate on basic management skills, business knowledge, values, and leadership ability.

Development Stage III.   This phase is for about 300 to 400 persons who are perceived as moving towards the top positions in GE. The development work includes advanced programs in financial management, human resources, information technology, and marketing. Also developed is the ability to work on a cross-functional basis.

Development Stage IV.   By this stage, the top performers have been "narrowed down" to 150. The program includes several month-long, intensive learning experiences in how to lead large, complex organizations.

Development Stage V.   Reserved for the fifty top executives who have made it to the corporate officer rank, this workshop, in which Welch participates, focuses on major business issues. The expectation is that action plans will be developed and implemented.

One might say that it is possible to trace the history of GE in the past three decades through the intensity of its concentration on executive development. During periods of high change within the organization and/or turbulence in the external environment, Crotonville became a mandatory experience. When the company was stable, attention to development ebbed somewhat.

Given Welch's aggressive style, emphasis on action and results, and ambitious vision, it is not surprising that the most recent brochure on the Management Development Institute closes with the following words:

> Crontonville will remain a unique competitive resource for the Company as long as it remains a major artery in the intellectual circulatory system

of GE and never allows its vision to stray from the real world. Crontonville, like the real world, is changing faster than ever.

And the changes that occur at Crontonville will have impacts on executive development throughout the world. How GE trains its executives and managers remains a model of how to approach development issues. Each year thousands of visitors come to Crontonville from all over the world. They ask, in a variety of languages, "What is your secret?"

Although the faculty and executive participants deny that there is a "secret," they do say that any marketplace success that GE has had— or will have—is due to the fact that from the day employees come to GE to the day they retire, they are never far from Crontonville, at least in spirit.

4 COMMUNICATING AND IMPLEMENTING A NEW CORPORATE STRATEGY AT XEROX

Few American corporations have undergone transformation in the decade of the eighties as profound as that of Xerox Corporation. The company entered the decade as the giant of the copier industry, but it had grown too lethargic and bureaucratic for its own good and was losing market share to the Japanese at an alarming rate. It exits the eighties as an office systems and financial services company that is perhaps the only large corporation to regain market share from the Japanese without the benefit of tariffs or any other form of government intervention.

The forces behind the dramatic turnaround are varied, complex, and not easy to define. Yet at least three things are certain. First, the change was masterminded and led by David T. Kearns, Xerox's chairman and chief executive officer. Second, Kearns used executive development as a key vehicle to introduce his strategic blueprint for the eighties and beyond. And third, Xerox considers itself a company that has profoundly and thoroughly changed, but that still has much to do.

In fact, Kearns is fond of saying, "Xerox is clearly in a period of transition. We are no longer the company that we once were and we are not yet the company that we must be." Central to that notion of transition is a change in the company's strategic direction. But why the need for change in the first place? To understand the answer to that question, it is necessary to first know something of the history of Xerox.

A RUDE AWAKENING

In March 1960, when the first Xerox copier was shipped to a Xerox customer, there were predictions that perhaps as many as 5000 units would be placed in three years. By the end of the year, some 10,000 orders had been placed, and Xerox was off and running. Revenues and profits grew routinely by 20 percent a year and more. It soon became clear that Xerox had created not merely a copier, but an entire new industry.

It was an industry that Xerox dominated for more than a decade. Revenues grew from $35 million in 1962 to more than $2 billion a decade later. The company seized the advantage of its head start on any potential competitor and set up worldwide manufacturing and marketing capabilities that made the term *Xerox* synonymous with *copy* in more than 100 countries in Latin America, Asia, Africa, and Europe.

It could not continue forever. And it didn't.

Those go-go days of the 1960s came to a gradual end during the 1970s. Perhaps the most important reason for the slowdown can be summarized in two interrelated words—cost and competition. In its heyday, Xerox paid little attention to cost and competition; it didn't have to. What little competition the corporation had was weak and fragmented. Consequently, Xerox could afford to price its products just about the way it wanted, and cost was not a major consideration for the management of the business.

Today more than 100 different companies make copying machines that compete directly with Xerox. The intensity of the competition is most evident in the low- and mid-volume copier market. By the company's own admission, "the stark fact is that the Japanese are producing machines with comparable copy quality and comparable reliability—and in some cases, they are doing it at less cost than Xerox. That allows the Japanese to price their products lower in the marketplace and forces Xerox to reduce its prices and lower its profits."

The result? Xerox market share dropped from a dominant position in the 1960s to less than 50 percent in 1980, at which time it was still slipping sharply. The rate of Xerox growth began to slip also. Consider this.

From the mid-1960s to the mid-1970s, Xerox revenues grew at an average annual rate of about 23 percent per year and profits increased at an average rate of about 20 percent. Between the mid-1970s and 1980, revenue growth slipped to an average annual rate of about 16 percent. During the same period, the average profit growth slipped to about 14 percent per year.

By 1980, the trend began to exhibit itself in a key measurement for the corporation—its return on assets. In 1980, ROA was a very healthy 19 percent. By 1983, it had plunged to 8.4 percent.

The downward trend was unmistakable and threatened to become a downward spiral. The precedent set by other large corporations in similar situations—most notably, the automotive industry—was not good. The pattern had been good growth, a dip in the rate of that growth, and then a plummet into a loss situation.

The Response to New Competitive Threats

Fortunately for Xerox, Kearns and his management team read the warning signals in time and began a major overhaul of the corporation in an effort to blunt the competitive threat. One of the first steps in the overhaul was to completely change the approach to product development and delivery by establishing a new corporate structure based on strategic business units. With this structure, different market segments could be addressed with different marketing strategies. One immediate effect of this change was that implementing the strategies, explained Kearns, "pushed a lot more decisionmaking a lot lower in the organization."

Another area subject to drastic change was personnel. Xerox was able to make substantial reductions in its cost base, but not without changing its benefits program and asking 1000 employees to leave. In Kearns's view, taking those steps involved breaking the "psychological contract" between Xerox management and employees, what he describes as "a nonbinding philosophy that said if you come to work for Xerox, we will take care of you and we will pay you better than anyone else. Given the realities of the marketplace, that was no longer possible. It was a question of making sacrifices or going out of business."

In fact, Xerox was finding that it could no longer take anything for granted, not even the market it had created. The reprography market had matured, and Xerox found itself at a crossroads: Should it continue to make new reprography products, or should it branch out into other markets, such as office systems and electronic printing? If the move into other markets was inevitable, how much of a presence should Xerox maintain in the reprography market it had dominated for so long?

These were not academic questions—Xerox had to find answers to them. But, according to Kearns, our senior people—and I mean the top 250 or so—had very uneven and even different understandings of these issues. I also had a concern that they didn't all appreciate the seriousness of the business situation. For instance, we wanted to introduce a major focus on improving our return on assets. I knew that would not be understood by some of our executives who had spent their entire careers chasing market shares.

THE SENIOR MANAGEMENT PROGRAM

Kearns established the Xerox Senior Management Program in 1983. In his mind, its mandate was "to communicate our strategic direction to the entire senior management team, to get their reaction and ideas and to make sure that we all understood the direction and were all marching to the beat of the same drummer."

This purpose was beyond the resources of the off-site management education program that Xerox had been participating in. For some time, the company had been sending its senior executives to a program run by Harvard Business School that focused on general management skills. Though the program was a good one, it was no longer enough. Xerox needed its own program, created especially to fill Xerox needs for executive development.

The internal training and development staff at Xerox was charged with the responsibility of designing the program. Their first step was to conduct interviews with the top twelve executives at Xerox to elicit their advice on a range of issues that included course content, program objectives, duration, attendees, structure, faculty, and approach.

"In retrospect," says Douglas Reid, senior vice president and senior staff officer of Xerox, "it was important to get the top twelve people involved from the beginning. They all had some strong opinions and sound ideas that were instrumental in the program that was eventually recommended. Several of them wound up as faculty members of the Senior Management Program and its strongest boosters. That might not have happened if we hadn't included them at the outset."

Several common themes emerged from these executive interviews:

- There was a clear need for the senior managers of Xerox to understand the company's total strategy and to understand the financial implications of that strategy so that they could develop a unified purpose, common goals, and consistent management style.

- There was a clear need to challenge senior managers to develop specific actions they would take themselves to implement the company's strategy.
- There was a clear need for senior managers to understand the critical success factors in each major business sector.

The training and development staff completed the design of the program in the fall of 1982. Entitled "Understanding and Implementing Xerox's Business Strategies," the Senior Management Program had five objectives:

- To clearly articulate and ensure the understanding of the business objectives and strategies of the corporation
- To give direction from top management regarding where Xerox was heading, how it planned to get there, and what participants had to do to ensure the success of the strategy
- To identify key opportunities and roadblocks in meeting the objectives and strategies, and to develop action plans for seizing opportunities, solving problems, and eliminating roadblocks
- To build teamwork across organizations and functions
- To state, clarify, and demonstrate the management style and practices desired at Xerox

That's a tall order. To accomplish it, Xerox packed a lot into a 5½-day program (see Figure 4–1). The curriculum began with a look at where Xerox had been and where it was heading. This included a thorough and candid presentation on the nature of the competitive threat worldwide. Participants were given a look at the world in 1992 and at the role that Xerox would like to play in that world. Finally, they were given a feel for the challenges they must overcome—particularly the financial hurdles—in order to achieve their long-term objectives for 1992 and beyond.

Examining the Corporate Strategy and Supporting Strategies

The next three segments of the program included a comprehensive overview of the corporate strategy, a detailed examination of the supporting strategies of each major business sector, and a discussion of the financial implications of the strategy, including a workshop on the importance of improving return on assets. Senior Xerox executives themselves

Figure 4–1. Xerox Senior Management Program.

MONDAY	TUESDAY	WEDNESDAY	THURSDAY	FRIDAY
• Program Introduction and Overview • Business Environment – 1992	• Information Resources Strategy • Systems Strategy	• Asset Management Workshop	• Leadership through Quality • Human Resource Issues	• Action Planning (Continued)
LUNCH	LUNCH	LUNCH	LUNCH	LUNCH
• Financial Condition and Implications • Corporate Strategic Direction	• Reprographics Strategy • Strategy Issues Workshop • Strategy Panel	• Technical Strategy • Customer Satisfaction Panel	• Management Practices • Action Planning	• Present & Discuss Issues • Closing Remarks • Program Summary
DINNER	DINNER	RECEPTION & DINNER WITH THE CUSTOMER	DINNER	
			• Action Planning (Continued)	

presented the material and led the discussions in these three segments. For example, the chief financial officer handled the session on the financial strategy and the workshop on return on assets, while the presidents of each major division discussed their strategies to support the corporate strategic direction.

"The ROA piece of the program," says Kearns,

> was almost vocational. Mel Howard [then chief financial officer and now vice chairman for financial services] gave an excellent primer at the beginning about return on assets, what its ingredients are, what drives it, its importance as a measurement, and so on. Later in the week, the Senior Management Program participants broke up into groups for a workshop. Each group made recommendations on what could be done to improve our ROA.

"Our people really learned a lot from the ROA workshop," recalled Reid.

> One of the recommendations [the participants] made was that a workshop on return on assets be developed for all Xerox people. As a result we developed a training-program and videotape on ROA improvement that got wide use. In fact, it's still being used in some parts of the organization. Hundreds of teams of Xerox people made improvements in the way they work in order to positively impact ROA. That simple recommendation and the resultant action paid for the Senior Management Program many times over.

After the ROA and business unit strategies had been discussed, the key functional strategies—including human resources and technology—were presented and discussed by the top executive in those functions. Doug Reid, then the corporate vice president of personnel, presented the human resource strategy to each of the twelve groups (about twenty-four executives in a class) that went through the Senior Management Program.

The communication in these sessions was very much two-way in nature and benefited not only the program participants but the presenters. According to Reid, this kind of give-and-take "was a very strong part of the program—getting direct feedback from your highest level managers from all over the world on their sense of priorities and what their needs were. It was a good interchange."

Reid recalled that one executive argued strongly for simply presenting the human resource strategy as a fait accompli and forgoing all the discussion. "We had had a history of debating our strategic direction to death and never locking in on one. So this person's argument was that the time for debate was over."

However pragmatic, that type of approach would not work at Xerox. Reid explained:

> People in Xerox . . . want to kick the tires on anything new and put their two cents' worth in. And we encourage that. We have a remarkably open environment which encourages people to be constructively critical of their management. That's a key plank in our culture, and one that's been good for us. It seemed counterproductive to suddenly say "Here's the strategy—accept it or leave."

Feedback on Management Style and Practice

Another section of the Xerox Senior Management Program dealt with management styles and practices. Prior to participating in the program, each executive was asked to give all of his or her direct reports a survey instrument that elicited their feedback on a series of management practices considered important to the executive's current set of responsibilities. The instrument also provided information on how executives ratings stacked up against those of their senior management peers. The feedback provided the basis for individual planning toward improving those areas that were most in need of change.

"It was a real eye-opener," says one executive who went through the program. "You think you're such a hotshot executive, and then you run smack into irrefutable evidence that says you have some glaring areas that need attention."

Says another: "It was all handled in a most professional way. It was totally anonymous. None of the other people in my class had the foggiest idea what my ratings were. And I got a great diagnostic tool that told me where I had to improve. I know that I changed parts of my management style as a result. Subsequent data indicates that my people think I've improved."

Listening to Customers

The section of the Senior Management Program on customer satisfaction was unique to American industry at that time. Senior representatives of a major Xerox customer were invited to give a panel presentation on what they liked and, perhaps more importantly, what they didn't like about Xerox. They were encouraged to emphasize the latter. Corporations invited for this purpose included the likes of Peat, Marwick, Mitchell & Company, Westinghouse, Digital Equipment Corporation, and Manufacturers Hanover Trust.

Each panel was chaired by a senior Xerox executive. Customers were asked to provide an overview of the "key contributors to your satisfaction *and* dissatisfaction with Xerox; your assessment of Xerox's products in terms of cost, quality, and reliability; and your recommendations on what Xerox must do to keep you as a major customer."

Discussions were candid and lively and lasted through a reception and dinner. The objective of the session was to put the senior executives of Xerox on the firing line. One senior executive explained what he got out of the discussions: "I have always been struck by Peter Drucker's insistence that management must make a conscious effort to get answers from the customer himself, rather than attempting to read his or her mind." That is precisely what the customer panel accomplished, in direct support of one of Xerox's major goals: "to significantly improve customer satisfaction."

A Contribution from Everyone— Including the CEO

The last section of the Xerox Senior Management Program was very much hands-on. Participants worked in small groups to identify a single important issue that they could act upon in order to make a positive contribution to achieving the corporate strategy. Although they were permitted to identify those parts of the effort that were beyond their control and would have to be addressed by the Corporate Management Committee, the clear emphasis was on coming up with actions and solutions whose implementation was totally within the power of an individual or group.

Each group then presented its findings and its action plan to the entire class for reactions and suggestions. Says one Xerox observer: "It's amazing how often the class would challenge the limitations the small group placed upon itself and point out that they had more authority than they gave themselves credit for. The small group would say it couldn't take a particular action. The larger group would ask why not and encourage them to go further."

The presentations to the class were actually dry runs. After polishing and refining them, each group presented its findings to Kearns, who spent a half-day listening and responding to the presentations. It was no mere exercise. Kearns directed that many of the presentations be given to the Corporate Management Committee or to a committee member with responsibility for the issue being addressed. Kearns often acted on some of these recommendations himself or directed that others do so.

Perhaps more important, Kearns used the sessions as a teaching vehicle. If a plank in the strategy seemed ambiguous or vague, he clarified it. If a legitimate concern was raised, he made sure it received proper attention and, if justified, action. One participant described Kearns's performance as nothing short of "inspirational." Said another, "[Kearns's participation] developed an openness and opportunity to share views, to have them heard, and to not be concerned that you would be labeled a nay-sayer if you raised an issue or voiced a criticism."

While taking nothing away from Kearns's extraordinary leadership, Doug Reid notes that such programs cannot succeed if the CEO is not closely involved.

> Without [Kearns's] ownership and recognition that it needed to be done, we never would have launched the program. The fact that David and the other senior executives actually taught in the program sent a strong message that this was not just another "nice-to-do-if-you-have-the-time" program. This was serious. It got 100 percent participation and commitment.

Kearns recalls participating in eleven of the twelve sessions. "I missed the one only because of a family commitment. The Senior Management Program was a priority on my calendar." He saw the importance of his participation as self-evident:

> Think about it. You had twenty-five executives in for a week—a really excellent group of people that might have come from a half-dozen countries. . . . They always included each major business function. Then your very top people exposed them to the corporation's strategic direction. And then on Friday afternoon, they gave you feedback.
>
> I had the opportunity to reshape the strategy if I thought they were right, to sell it, to gain their ownership and commitment. If that's not critical work for the CEO, then you tell me what is.
>
> But it was also fun. . . . The sessions were so much better for me than going through those sessions where people ask general questions or raise broad issues. These workshops were focused, they had to raise and then say what they were going to *do* about it or what they wanted me to do about it. That made it all very real and very proactive.

Importing Lessons in Quality from Fuiji Xerox

One last element of the Xerox Senior Management Program deserves more than just a few words of explanation. During the period between 1980 and the start of the Senior Management Program in early 1983, Xerox had been making significant progress in its competitive battle against the Japanese abroad and against IBM and Kodak at home. The Series 10 line of copiers had been introduced and had been extremely well received in the marketplace. Entry into electronics-based technology—such as electronic printing and the Memorywriter line of electronic typewriters—was also doing well.

But Kearns realized that "doing well" was not enough. In the few years prior to 1983, he had visited Japan some twenty-two times and had gained enormous respect for the management skill of the Japanese in general, and the skill of Fuiji Xerox in particular.

Following its founding in 1962, Fuiji Xerox had experienced a period of phenomenal growth. Like its parent, it had a head start in the emerging copier industry and very little competition. In 1975, the bubble burst. Japan's economy was jolted by the worldwide oil crisis. Competition from both Richo and Canon became a harsh fact of life. And Fuiji Xerox lacked adequate products with which to respond. Sales began to slip, and it soon became apparent that, unless something bold was done, the very survival of the company was threatened.

In May of 1976, Fuiji Xerox announced that it was launching a total quality process under the name New Xerox Movement. The company's objectives were to develop new products to satisfy market requirements, to strengthen the marketing organization, to bring costs under control throughout the company, and to introduce new basic technologies.

The organization responded with enthusiasm and commitment. Quality circles flourished. The use of statistical tools to improve quality at all levels became the norm. Teamwork was fostered and rewarded. The entire Fuiji Xerox family of operating companies, subsidiaries, and suppliers was brought into the New Xerox Movement. A participative management style was nurtured. And an absolute dedication to quality improvement and cost reduction became an accepted way of life.

The turnaround was nothing short of phenomenal—what one observer has called "the greatest comeback since Lazarus." In 1978, Fuiji Xerox launched the very successful Xerox 3500 copier. In 1980, Japan's highly coveted National Deming Award was bestowed on Fuiji Xerox. And by 1982, revenues were increasing at an annual rate of 25 percent, and profits by 28 percent. Much of the success was attributed to the New Xerox Movement, in which Kearns became an unabashed believer.

In February of 1982, Kearns assembled the top twenty-five Xerox executives for a two-day meeting to begin to plan a total, worldwide quality strategy. "At that meeting," says one participant, "David made it very, very clear that we were beginning something major, that he wanted and needed our help, and that only one thing was not debatable: Xerox was going to have a total quality process and strategy."

At the end of the meeting, a blue ribbon, 15-person task force was put together to develop a strategy that eventually was called Leadership Through Quality. This strategy was shared with each Senior Management Program class, and the feedback of participants was sought.

Says Kearns: "They really went at it in these sessions. This helped us shape the strategy. Just as important, when Leadership Through Quality was launched in early 1984, our top 300 or so executives had touched it and felt at least some degree of ownership. I'm convinced that this was an important factor in its early acceptance and success."

ASSESSMENTS OF THE PROGRAM

Between March of 1983 and January of 1984, twelve sessions of the Senior Management Program were conducted. In all, 288 senior managers attended. Participants included all the officers of the corporation, all the functional heads, and the heads of all major operating organizations.

Feedback on the program was extremely positive. One participant probably spoke for many when he wrote: "The program provided a believable and comprehensible picture of where the corporation is now in total and where it is heading. It was frank, to the point, and provided a good realization that our problems will be tough but not impossible to resolve. I understand what I have to do and I am committed to get out and do it."

That type of response was, of course, exactly what Xerox had hoped for. At first, however, it had seemed like far too much to hope for. Kearns remembers that "we almost abandoned the whole darn thing after the first class." Like any pilot project venturing into uncharted territory, it was plagued at first with the sour reactions of the type of person who, in Kearns's words, would tell you that Rembrandt was a lousy painter or that Babe Ruth couldn't hit worth a damn. Well, some of the people in this first class really tore the Senior Management Program apart. And some of them went back and told their leaders, the presidents of the operating groups, that it was awful and should be cancelled. That scared the leaders, and some of them wanted to pull the plug on the program.

Fortunately, a second group went through the program before a decision was made. These participants thought the program so worthwhile that, according to Kearns, "they said no matter what you do, *don't* cancel it. . . . So we persevered, and I never regretted it."

Doug Reid feels that the program achieved all of its original objectives. It communicated the overall strategy to everyone concerned (that is, the entire top management team), and it accomplished related goals such as providing executives with feedback on their management style, feedback they needed if they were to be full participants in steering Xerox in its new direction.

But perhaps the most important unexpected benefit was having the strategy sharpened and fine-tuned as it would never have been without the frank and intensive discussions in the Senior Management Program. For instance, top management discovered that many executives had an inadequate grasp of the systems business. A major overhaul in systems training for managers was instituted and has been very effective. The company's communication strategy was also reviewed and subsequently revised to create greater consistency in the way Xerox communicates with its various constituencies: employees, shareholders, customers, the press, and so on.

But the fine-tuning wasn't confined to top mangement. According to Reid, "It also was a catalyst for senior managers to rethink their own strategies. A lot of key managers . . . said [to themselves], 'Wait a minute, not only should I communicate the overall business strategy to my people, but I better make sure mine ties to it, and I better do that as a regular part of my own management job.' "

To other companies contemplating an executive education program like Xerox's, David Kearns recommends

a little faith and patience. . . . You don't implement corporate strategies overnight. . . . So you can't expect results overnight. There's no doubt in my mind that we moved out faster on ROA and some other pieces of the strategy. And there's no doubt in my mind that our strategy is sounder and more focused because of the work we did back in 1983. It takes time for those things to show up on the balance sheet. But the results do come.

Xerox is testimony to that. Its return on assets has been on a steady upswing since 1983 and has returned to double-digit levels. Revenue and profit are showing steady growth.

Nor is Xerox content to rest with its recent successes. The company's new president, Paul A. Allaire, is a firm believer in management training and development. One Xerox professional says, "Management training and development has always been important in Xerox. Kearns continued that legacy by making executive education a competitive tool. Now it's becoming clear that Allaire intends to make it an even more potent weapon."

III GLOBAL COMPETITION

5 A MATTER OF SURVIVAL: MOTOROLA MEETS THE JAPANESE CHALLENGE

Asia. The Pacific Rim. Japan, Inc. The words strike fear into the hearts of many an American business executive. And with good reason.

A mere generation ago, the Japanese accounted for only 2 percent of the world's economy. Today, Japan claims 10 percent, and they have done it largely at the expense of the United States. In the short span of three years, the United States has gone from being the largest *creditor* nation in the world, to the largest *debtor* nation. Some twenty-five years ago, America controlled 35 percent of the world economy. Today, our portion is barely 20 percent.

A few additional facts underscore the economic strength that has been built up in Asia. Consider these:

- In *Fortune*'s listing of the largest 500 non-U.S. industrial corporations, 146 are Japanese.
- Twenty-eight of the 100 largest commercial banks outside of the United States—including the top four—are Japanese.
- Toyota and Nissan have clawed their way to third and fourth position in the ranks of automotive companies, behind General Motors and Ford.
- Nippon Steel is larger than U.S. Steel.
- Hitachi and Matsushita Electric are second and third in size to General Electric, and larger than Siemens and Philips.

And so the list goes on. The point is painfully clear. Led by the Japanese, Asia is at one and the same time an ominous threat and an expansive market for American business. Perhaps no other major American corporation is waging a more aggressive war against global competition than Motorola, Inc.—the $8 billion-a-year high-technology giant headquartered in Schaumberg, Illinois. The commander-in-chief is none other than Robert W. Galvin, Motorola's Chairman of the Board and son of the corporation's founding father.

EXECUTIVE EDUCATION ON THE FRONT LINES

Galvin's war is being waged on at least three major fronts. The first two are not surprising; the third is.

The first is an all-out attack on Japan's trading practices. He charges that American business is being forced to move manufacturing operations abroad because of unfair competition from Asia, and he has been an outspoken advocate of government intervention. "By failing to stand up for American industry," Galvin charges, "the American government is inadvertently letting American industry walk out on this society."

"We think the issue is serious," Galvin continues, "and we believe that we must step into the breach when we see that it hasn't been filled. We can't defer the responsibility to someone else."

Nor is Galvin content to blunt the Japanese threat through rhetoric and lobbying efforts alone. The second front of Galvin's war is a massive restructuring of Motorola. Gone are the days when Motorola's strength was derived from electronic consumer products. The metamorphosis at Motorola has produced some surprising results. At the end of 1983, for example, the company built its last car radio.

Motorola's market strength today is built on a three-pronged strategy of continuing domestic dominance in the growing market for two-way radio frequency communications, strengthening its capabilities in distributed data processing, and building a relatively new but already highly successful semiconductor business. Communications now account for about 40 percent of Motorola's sales, and semiconductors for another 35 percent.

The third—and somewhat surprising—front of Galvin's campaign against global competition is what he calls "our most driving force, our culture of renewal." The centerpiece of this "culture of renewal" is an executive education strategy aimed at the top 200 corporate officers.

"American business—and Motorola people are no exception—doesn't fully understand the scope and the nature of global competitiveness," argues Galvin. "The intensity and the quality of the threat from Asia is underestimated and misunderstood. We've been thinking and talking about Japan for years, but we never really zeroed in on the nature of the threat and what our strategic response ought to be."

Galvin has a reputation in industry as a leading champion of executive development. At least part of the credit for that goes to his father. "He started educating me when I was an adolescent," says Galvin.

The talk around the dinner table centered on the day's activities at the office. When I was a little older, he used to give me drafts of his speeches to read and react to. Often my suggestions would work their way into the final speech. When I was only seventeen, he made it clear that someday I would take the reins from him. At a meeting of Motorola distributors at the Edgewater Beach Hotel in Chicago, he pointed to me and said, "Some of you have asked me about the future. I want to introduce you to the future. I want you to meet my son." That's a moment I will never forget. From that moment on, my education began in earnest, and it continued throughout my career with Motorola.

A few weeks after Galvin's introduction to the distributors, he began to work in the stockroom of the Motorola plant on Augusta Boulevard. That was 18 June 1940. On Friday of the third week, Galvin recalls that he thought he knew everything there was to know about the stockroom and was going to tell his supervisor that he was ready to move on to a new assignment.

But I could never quite get him alone to tell him. By Monday, I had thought it over and decided not to say anything. As the weeks grew into months, I discovered something. The stockroom was far more complex than I had ever imagined. I left at the end of the summer realizing that I still had a lot to learn about that stockroom.

I never forgot that experience and I don't let my executives forget it either. We are all prone to think we know more than we do. That's especially true when we reach higher levels of responsibility. If we're not careful, we can become a little insulated, a little complacent, a little arrogant about how much—or how little—we know.

This attitude was at least partially responsible for Motorla's establishing a world-class executive development program. Throughout the 1960s and into the early 1970s, the Motorola Executive Institute brought groups of sixteen executives at a time into a retreat in Arizona. These programs usually lasted an entire month.

The faculty consisted of some of the most renowned and respected academics from around the world. The intent was to stimulate the thinking and broaden the perspective of Motorola's cadre of senior managers. This approach worked well enough in the 1960s, but by the early 1970s the world had begun to change dramatically. It was becoming increasingly apparent that the much-discussed global economy was fast becoming a reality. That had both pluses and minuses for Motorola. The plus was the opening up of entire new markets for products. The minus was the dramatic intensification of competition. Motorola wasn't ready for either.

"In an environment like that," says Galvin, "30-day education programs in the Arizona desert suddenly seemed inappropriate. They were nice things to do, but no longer seemed necessary. And we could no longer afford things that weren't necessary."

There's an irony here. Global competition and the need to become more cost-effective led to the demise of the Motorola Executive Institute in the mid-1970s. These same forces led Motorola to begin executive education programs again in the 1980s.

The irony can be explained away, however, by a look at the evolution of Motorola. The company was founded as a producer of radio products for consumers: car radios, walkie-talkies, transistors, transponders, and tabletop televisions. But in the 1970s, Motorola started changing over from consumer products to high-tech industrial electronics: cellular telephones, modems, and microprocessors. The company progressed to producing automated office systems, display pagers, and 32-bit microprocessors in the 1980s and will be in the forefront of the semiconductor industy in the 1990s, producing the kind of integrated circuits that allow robots to see and computers to talk.

"In the environment we're in," explains Galvin, " 'technological obsolescence' is more than just a buzzword. It's a fact of life that we have to manage if we are to continue to be successful *and* fair to our employees. When I began to realize this, I directed that a major study be undertaken to determine what our total training needs would be in the future."

Galvin reasoned that Motorola had emerged as a very different corporate entity over the past decade and had proven itself to be an organization capable of great change and adaptability. As industries, technologies, and competitors evolved, Motorola had the inner strength to keep up, even keep ahead.

Galvin recognized that this evolution was likely to accelerate—that it would involve what Columbia University's Charles Frankel once called "change in the tempo of change itself." Motorola's future—like that of any world-class competitor—will depend on its continued ability to sense the direction of change, recognize and select from among its available options, and adjust its own direction accordingly. Sensing the change and recognizing the options are forms of vision.

THE MOTOROLA SENIOR EXECUTIVE PROGRAM

In late 1982, Galvin directed the professional training and development staff to develop and implement what would be the Senior Executive Program. This program is intended to build Motorola's long-term strength and global competitiveness by enhancing the vision of the officers. The program is a long-term educational process that has two overriding objectives:

- To increase senior executives' knowledge, awareness, and understanding of future external trends and environments and their potential impact on—as well as opportunities for—Motorola
- To enhance the ability of senior executives to collectively influence Motorola's future in light of anticipated and sweeping change

"In our judgment," says Bill Wiggenhorn, who's in charge of the program, "it was not feasible to examine the changing nature of competition on a worldwide basis in one fell swoop, so we began by designing a program for 1984 that dealt exclusively with Asia." The program had three objectives:

- To identify and understand key, emerging competitive threats in Asia
- To understand the key factors in Asia that are subject to change and may affect Motorola's business
- To provide a perspective that would be helpful in the development and improvement of strategic plans in the respective business units

"In retrospect," says Wiggenhorn, "one of the things we did particularly well in designing the program on Asia was including senior managers in the development process." Nearly eighty of the 150 corporate officers who would eventually participate in the program were interviewed. With one exception, each of them strongly supported the need for a program, and there was a clear consensus that the subject matter should deal with global competition in general, and with Asia in particular.

A board of advisors—a group of senior managers at Motorola who had provided direction on management training in the past—was heavily involved in developing the program. They proved to be an invaluable resource, adding their counsel and experience at key junctures in the program development cycle. For example, the training and development staff prepared a request for proposals for the development of a "turn-key" program. Fifteen firms—many of them among the best in the training and development field—sent in proposals. The board of advisors rejected all of them.

They argued that the programs were either off-the-shelf or adapted from other programs. What was needed was a program designed from the ground up with Motorola in mind. The board directed that the management training staff develop the program internally with the assistance of outside consultants.

"That decision," says Wiggenhorn, "spelled the difference between success and failure. It assured us that the program would be right on target for Motorola."

The board also influenced and strengthened the focus of the program. The Management Training Advisory Committee (Board of Advisors) was persistent in its advice that the program focus primarily on competitors rather than on market opportunities and/or culture and history.

What emerged, with the full endorsement and commitment of top management, was an intensive 6-day program aimed specifically at Motorola. The key 200 executives in the company participated in groups of twenty. The first group included Galvin himself. In a statement signed by Galvin, Vice Chairman and Chief Operating Officer William J. Weisz, and President John Mitchell, there was no doubt as to the importance and the purpose these officers attached to the Senior Executive Program.

They wrote, "The program offers an opportunity for each of us to carry on a responsibility that is fundamental to the continued well-being of Motorola. Throughout the week and long after we return to our businesses, we need to relentlessly challenge the assumptions on which we have come to rely while leading this corporation."

To say that the six-day seminar was fast-paced and information-laden would be an understatement. It began with an overview of the position of the United States in a worldwide economy that has become increasingly competitive, a discussion of the nature and value of a global perspective, and an examination of Motorola's presence and activities in Asia.

Analysis and discussion by organization and country followed. The aim was to give Motorola executives a common perspective, framework, and language with which to assess the relative strengths and weaknesses of various Asian countries, as well as those of competitors in that part of the world.

Once they had that background, participants proceeded to examine the major economic entities in Asia of interest to Motorola: China, Japan, Southeast Asia, Taiwan, and South Korea. Economic, political, and social factors were considered in each country analysis.

A variety of experts—usually drawn from the academic community—made presentations and led the discussion of each country. While each country expert held forth in the front of the room, a second expert—often drawn from the ranks of the State Department, and always someone who had lived in the country under discussion—sat in the back of the room playing devil's advocate, that is, challenging and adding real-world examples to the discussion. The presence of this second expert ensured that the academic experts neither digressed nor got too theoretical.

That blend of the viewpoints of the academic and the seasoned field professional added a special and powerful ingredient to the country analysis. It stimulted and encouraged dialogue and discussion and added tremendous credibility to the entire program. Participants came away with a much richer understanding of each country.

The faculty assembled for the Senior Executive Program brought some very impressive credentials to their task. There was Mike Oksenburg from the University of Michigan, head of their Center for China Studies Department, and author of many books on China, Professor Yu Sang Chang of Boston University's School of Management and founder of the Asian Management Center, Dick Sneider, a former ambassador to Korea, and a variety of other Asian experts. They came from the Departments of State and Commerce, from Harvard, MIT, Columbia, Berkeley, and the University of Michigan, and from the Rand Corporation, the American Enterprise Institute, and the Center for Policy Alternatives.

They were, in short, the best and the brightest. They combined the wisdom of academia with vast practical experience gained from consulting with the government and large corporations and from living abroad. Perhaps more importantly, they were comfortable dealing with corporate executives, they listened well, and they enjoyed the debate and dialogue cultivated by the Senior Executive Program.

But the data and judgments offered by the experts were of little practical use unless they could be properly read and interpreted by Motorola's executives. This kind of literacy requires familiarity with the language and concepts of economists, social scientists, and geopolitical experts and with the institutional arrangements of different countries, alliances, and international agencies. For example, precisely what does an economist mean by *GNP*? How does the Chinese banking system function? How does the International Monetary Fund affect Taiwan?

With answers to questions like these, the data could then be organized in a way that would result in sound conclusions and rational decisions about the future shape of national economies. A process developed by Professor Bruce Scott of Harvard was used during the Senior Executive Program to answer five basic questions that would help participants assimilate all the information being presented to them.

1.   What are this country's economic strategies, goals, and trade and investment policies?
2.   Is this country's economic performance in accord with its goals and with the international context?
3.   Can this country's economic policies bring about change in order to coordinate its actual economic performance?
4.   Is it reasonable to expect that these national policy changes will occur and that they will positively impact the peformance of this country's economy?
5.   What forces will shape the future domestic and international environment affecting this country, and what likelihood is there that its government will be able to manage the challenges these new forces present?

A major feature of the program was a workshop aimed at examining a major Motorola competitor in Asia. To most participants, that close look at a real, flesh-and-blood competitor took the Senior Executive Program completely out of the realm of the academic and riveted their attention on the real world. There is nothing abstract about examining a known, major competitor who is selling real products to what could be your customers.

Once the country-by-country analysis and the analysis of Motorola's major competitor in Asia were completed, the focus of each group turned inward. The class broke up into smaller groups of approximately five to seven executives. They reviewed the entire week and summarized and synthesized what had been learned. Then they identified and prioritized the key issues for Motorola and recommended specific action plans to deal with them.

THE PROGRAM AT WORK: TAKING ACTION

On the final day of the program, the recommendations were presented to one of the top three executives in Motorola—Galvin, Weisz, or Mitchell. These sessions were no mere classroom exercises. They were serious business discussions and the culmination of a week's introspection and education. Perhaps most importantly, they took place away from the "heat of battle." Somehow, in this setting, the discussions were more creative and less tied to considerations of turf and this quarter's bottom line.

Examples of specific actions that resulted from these recommendations include:

- Review and alteration of Motorola's strategic assumptions about manufacturing offshore
- Reconsideration of Motorola's approach to global competition by a task force composed of six senior managers (all division presidents relieved of their normal responsibilities for the 3½-month duration of the task force)
- Establishment of a new international organization at the corporate level with a charter to further rethink and, if necessary, reorganize the way Motorola competes globally

Participant reaction to the program was extraordinarily positive:

Programs like this are a key to our survival.

Going into the program, I thought it was six days I couldn't afford to take away from the office. Coming out of the program, I realized it was six days I couldn't afford to miss.

The program was outstanding—an essential training experience for every senior-level executive.

Some 98 percent of the participants voted to continue and expand the program. Bill Wiggenhorn—now a Motorola vice president and corporate officer—says that the success of the program was due to a convergence

of many things, including "Bob Galvin's leadership [and] the involvement of senior executives in the program's design, targeting it specifically
to Motorola. But if I had to zero in on just one specific, it would have
to be that the content was right for its time."

Wiggenhorn admits that Motorola very possibly would have implemented some of the actions that came out of the Senior Executive
Program even if it hadn't taken place.

> First, it accelerated the actions by focusing the attention of the entire senior
> management team on the threat and the opportunity in Asia. And second,
> the program developed a high degree of consensus on what had to be done.
> If a few people at the top had made these same decisions, a lot of people
> might have second-guessed them. This way, everyone was heard, everyone
> participated in making recommendations, and everyone felt good about the
> outcome.

Motorola's Asian strategy appears to be working well. The company's
growth rate in Asia has increased substantially, and its performance is
significantly better than that of its competitors. With those kinds of
results, it's easy to understand why Motorola has pushed ahead with
its executive education programs.

In 1986, Motorola brought the program on Asia to some 3000 upper-
middle managers around the world. The program was given in fourteen locations and taught by Motorola executives. Like its predecessor,
it was well received and highly successful.

In 1987, Motorola identified "cycle times" as a major issue. "Cycle
times" is usually understood to refer to product development. Motorola,
however, broadened its thinking to include *all* cycle times—everything
from the time it takes to bill customers to the time it takes to hire people. "World-class competitors," says Wiggenhorn, "will have to react
quickly to change. That means shorter cycle times. Consequently, the
1987 program focused on that issue."

And 1988? The focus is on the customer in the years 2000 and 2050
and what those customers will want from Motorola. "That," says Wiggenhorn, "will lead us, I'm sure, to the subjects of still more executive
education programs for the future."

Wiggenhorn has the following advice for anyone starting up a similar
program:

> First, before you design any programs, set up a steering committee of
> representatives of the targeted group. Let them identify their needs and in-
> terests. Second, make sure you have someone on staff, or hire a consultant,

who can assess the outside talent and efforts you will need. Third, enlist the top of the house to play two critical roles—go through the program themselves and teach part of the program. Fourth, take minutes of the recommendations of each class, and make them available to subsequent classes so they can build on them. And fifth, use outside consultants as appropriate, but manage the program internally.

Maybe I would add a sixth: charge back the cost of the program to the budget center of each participant. A good senior executive program is neither a retreat nor a finishing school. It should be valuable enough that the training and development function can legitimately charge for it, and it should provide sufficient value so that the participant doesn't mind paying.

Bob Galvin seems to agree with this last suggestion. Asked how he feels about the Motorola Senior Executive Program that he set in motion back in 1982, Galvin says, "We realized the return on our investment on the 1984 Senior Executive Program long before the last of the nine groups of officers had completed the program."

George M.C. Fisher is the new CEO at Motorola. Like Galvin, he is dedicated to corporate education and training in general, and to executive education in particular. In fact, Fisher was an active member of the program's board of advisors. A self-described "education fanatic," Fisher is committed to the continued use of executive education as a key tool in keeping Motorola competitive around the world.

6 EMHART: FROM A DOMESTIC COMPANY TO A GLOBAL COMPETITOR

It's hard to pick up the business section of your daily newspaper or a business journal today without reading about the globalization of world markets, the rapid rate of industrialization of the Third World, or dramatic shifts in trading patterns that had remained relatively stable since World War II. Asia, for example, is a formidable competitive power that has already become the world leader in several industries and is threatening to in many others. But the sheer size of the region also makes it an attractive outlet for American products, as well as a potential manufacturing and sourcing base.

What is perhaps less well known is that other parts of the world are also coming of economic age. Western Europe has rebounded strongly from its slump of the seventies and is once again producing quality products for export. And Latin America—despite its enormous inflation and debt—has dramatically improved and expanded its manufacturing and production capabilities.

Marshall McLuhan's prediction of a global village is upon us. The economies of New York and London, Los Angeles and Tokyo, Dallas and Rio de Janeiro are intertwined. That truism has been well documented and will hardly come as news to the reader. What is news, however, is the extent to which executive development has become a key plank in the strategies of some leading corporations—such as Motorola—in their attempts to become more competitive in global markets themselves.

Another case in point is Emhart Corporation. Headquartered in Farmington, Connecticut, Emhart is a multinational corporation that manufactures and markets a variety of products on a worldwide basis, with operations in some thirty countries—principally in the United States and Europe, but also in Latin America. With revenues in the neighborhood of $2 billion a year, Emhart's return on average shareholder's equity has been running at a very healthy 17 percent for the past few years.

The Emhart product line is long and varied. It includes hardware, fasteners, store equipment, adhesive systems, smoke, heat, and burglary detection devices, shoe manufacturing machinery, and much more. Since 1979, Emhart has embarked on a thoughtful and strategic acquisition program that has brought more than twenty modest-sized companies into the Emhart fold.

Most recently, Emhart has expanded into the high-technology market. In December of 1986, it acquired Planning Research Corporation of McLean, Virginia, the prime contractor on a $300 million contract to automate the U.S. Patent and Trademarket Office. Planning Research also services a nationwide network for multiple listing real estate operators. In October of 1987, Emhart bought Advanced Technology, Inc. of Reston, Virginia, a privately held company with a range of government computer service contracts, including work on the Strategic Defense Initiative, or "Star Wars."

LOOKING ABROAD FOR NEW MARKETS

Peter L. Scott, chairman and chief executive officer of Emhart, said that the acquisitions were part of a strategic plan to develop a new business sector—information and electronic systems. Emhart estimates revenues of $700 million from its new sector in 1988.

The reason for the lastest diversification? Despite its enviable and steady growth, Emhart's product line is essentially mature. Future growth must come, in at least some measure, from beyond American shores. And a sophisticated product like information and electronic systems is more likely to find worldwide markets. Fortunately for Emhart, its chairman and chief executive officer until his retirement in 1986, T. Mitchell Ford, recognized this:

> It is important to resist analyzing Emhart's operations on a U.S. or domestic basis only. Granted, what is close at hand is the most familiar and most reported. But, in our case, this can be misleading. Roughly half of our

revenue already comes from outside the United States, and the markets for our products that are growing the most rapidly are all outside the United States.

The fact had not escaped Emhart's general managers. According to Steve Ruffi, vice chairman and CAO at the time:

> We were receiving almost daily proposals, memos, and telephone calls with ideas and requests to become more aggressive in international markets. Our challenge was not in motivating our senior managers, but rather in bringing rational decisionmaking and focus to our global expansion initiatives. We probably could have developed a sensible strategy on our own here at headquarters, but no one would have paid attention. It was important that our top sixty people immerse themselves in global strategic issues.

The Emhart executives chose executive education as the vehicle for making this happen. This choice was not surprising because Emhart has a long tradition of providing education and development experiences for its senior managers, who were among the first and most frequent attendees at academic seminars and programs for corporate executives sponsored by Harvard and other leading business schools.

Biennially, Emhart convenes a 2-day worldwide conference for its senior executives to explore contemporary issues and major trends that may have an impact on their business in the future. For example, in 1982 seven world-recognized leaders in economics, communications, human resources, technology, education, and global politics discussed the changing values, priorities, and attitudes shaping the eighties. Speakers included the Honorable Edward Heath, former prime minister of Great Britain, Theodore L. Eliot, Jr., dean of the Fletcher School of Law and Diplomacy, Richard Bodman, then president of COMSAT General, and Dr. Jacob Goldman, former chief scientist of Xerox Corporation.

In 1984, a group of similar expertise examined changes in society and the profound impact they will have on the management of resources in the years ahead. This group included Librarian of Congress Daniel Boorstin, Glen E. Watts, president of the Communications Workers of America, former Deputy Secretary of Commerce Sidney Harmon, and John Diebold, the renowned technocrat who coined the word *automation*.

According to Ford, these conferences had always been well received by Emhart managers. "That led me to pursue the idea of doing something similar as a way of educating our executives on globalization and as a first step in bringing more focus and purpose to our overseas expansion strategies."

THE 1985 EXECUTIVE EDUCATION PROGRAM

As a first step, an outside consultant was asked to develop a concept paper for Emhart's senior management. See Figure 6–1, which is an excellent snapshot of an executive education program in its early design stages. Refinements were made and the content adjusted until Ford and the other key executives were in agreement.

What developed was the Executive Education Program, which focused on the theme of global competitiveness and was conducted in 1985. The program had five objectives:

- To assist Emhart in making the transition from being a domestic-oriented company to a global competitor
- To encourage the development of a global business perspective among Emhart's senior executives
- To identify the factors critical to successfully competing in global markets
- To assess Emhart's global competitive position and determine actions to improve it
- To encourage the sharing of ideas and experiences and the building of sound working relationships and teamwork

Three 5½-day programs were held in May, September, and November of 1985. Each was attended by twenty of Emhart's sixty most senior executives. The morning of the first day focused on the nature and value of a global perspective and involved an examination of the differences between domestic and global businesses and the importance to the future success of Emhart of becoming global. That was followed by half-day sessions on key forces in the global environment in the year 2000, American competitiveness in the world economy, the dynamics of global trade, global marketing, sourcing, design, and manufacturing, and operational issues unique to global business, such as government regulations and organizational structure.

A related issue addressed in the course of the seminar was the existence of cultural differences in different areas of the world, especially those impacting business operations and practices in various countries.

The working sessions were supplemented by generous doses of homework, including both reading and planning exercises. The faculty was drawn from The Futures Group, MIT, the Economic Development

Figure 6-1. Emhart 1985 Executive Education Program, "Global Competitiveness"—Overview.

OVERALL NEEDS	PROGRAM CONCEPT	PROGRAM OBJECTIVES	SUBJECT MATTER
• To broaden and strengthen Emhart's key management resources • To provide a continuing forum for management interchange and the exchange of ideas/experiences to build working relationships and foster teamwork • To review and reinforce the knowledge and skills required for success	• A 5-1/2 day Executive Education Program to provide: – The practical competencies necessary to successfully compete in the world marketplace – A global business perspective essential to success in a world business environment • A program design which requires: – The interchange of ideas and information among executives – Cross-divisional/functional cooperation and coordination – The application of new competencies to the development of individual and business action plans	• Assist Emhart in making the transition from a successful domestic company to a successful global competitor • Encourage the development of a global perspective in managing Emhart and each business unit • Foster an understanding of key factors in the external environment and their implications for Emhart • Assess Emhart's global competitive position and recommend actions to further develop and improve this position • Review and reinforce competencies required for the effective management of a competitive global enterprise and encourage on-the-job application • Provide a continuing forum for management interchange, building working relationships across divisions, establishing networks, sharing experiences and developing teamwork	• The Nature and Value of a Global Perspective • The World in the Year 2000 • Global Competitive Trends • The Dynamics of Global Trade • Global Sourcing, Design and Manufacturing • Cultural Differences • Global Markets/Marketing • Operational Issues in a Global Business • Global Competitiveness: Critical Success Factors • Conclusions and Implications

Institute of the World Bank, the Harvard Business School, other companies, and the Office of the U.S. Trade Representative, among other organizations.

A highlight of the program occurred towards the end. The full group identified and discussed the critical success factors that distinguish successful global competitors from unsuccessful ones. To facilitate that discussion, a research paper produced specifically for the Emhart program was given to the participants. It identified ten success factors, which are shown in Figure 6-2.

Program participants were asked to assess their individual business units as well as the total company against these criteria. Then they developed personal plans to improve their business unit strategies. Later, they broke up into three subgroups to make specific recommendations to one of Emhart's top three executives on what the company needed to do to improve its global competitiveness.

Ruffi gave some indication of his high expectations for the program when he kicked off the first session with these words:

Figure 6–2. Emhart Executive Education Program:
Ten Success Factors for the Global Competitor.

1. Successful global competitors perceive themselves as multinational, understand the implications of that for their business, and are led by a management that is comfortable in the world arena.

2. Successful global competitors develop an integrated and innovative worldwide strategy that preempts others from competing, or makes it very difficult and costly to do so.

3. Successful global competitors aggressively and effectively implement their worldwide strategy and back it with large investments.

4. Successful global competitors understand that technological innovation is no longer confined to the United States and have developed systems for tapping technological innovation abroad.

5. Successful global competitors operate as though the world were one large market, not a series of individual countries.

6. Successful global competitors have developed an organization structure that is well thought out and unique to their own business.

7. Successful global competitors have a system to keep abreast of political changes abroad and the implications for their business.

8. Successful global competitors recognize the need to make their management team international and have a system in place to accomplish the goal.

9. Successful global competitors provide their outside directors with an active role in the affairs of the company.

10. Successful global competitors are well-managed.

Because of our heavy involvement in global businesses, we should be smarter than others in this business environment. If we are smarter, we should continue to maintain or increase our present global position in spite of growing competition and make strategic penetration in new, attractive regional markets.

Short-term management policies may have been adequate prior to the '80s, but now we must predict the major changes which lie ahead and provide the strategic leadership necessary for the long-term success of the company.

He wasn't disappointed.

Overall satisfaction with the program was highly rated by the participants. According to one participant, the program was "reminiscent of the best management programs at the Harvard Business School." But the real indication of its value was in the steps Emhart took as a direct result of the seminar. This partial list gives a good idea of the breadth and impact of the actions taken:

- The corporate mission statement was revised to reflect Emhart's commitment to global markets.
- A Far East strategy was developed, presented to Emhart's board of directors, and approved.
- A pricing task force was formed and given a broad charter to develop an intercompany pricing policy, which was subsequently implemented.
- A Pacific Basin technology task force was formed and has already identified a half-dozen opportunities for Emhart that are being actively pursued.

Just as important as these hard, tangible results of the program was the more subjective impact it had on the participants. Says one:

It was a real eye-opener, but not just in the sense you might have anticipated. Yes, it made us more intimately aware of the nature of the opportunities overseas, but it also made us more aware that you couldn't jump in with both feet. The opportunities abroad are also fraught with risk. Many of us knew that, of course, but the seminar brought some of those risks into sharper focus.

"That kind of reaction is precisely what we wanted," says William C. Lichtenfels, then chief operating officer.

Our executives know a great deal about globalization. Some of them manage large organizations in places like Brazil and throughout Western Europe.

A lot of them were pushing us at headquarters to go in this or that direction. You would get no argument from any of our executives against doing *something*. But precisely what and how much we should do was hotly debated.

THE 1986 EXECUTIVE EDUCATION PROGRAM

Ford, Ruffi, and Lichtenfels were so pleased with the results of the first program that they immediately gave a green light to planning a second. Not surprisingly, they mandated that it follow the same general format and that it zero in on the world's largest growth opportunity: the Pacific Basin.

As with the 1985 program, a consultant was brought in to provide a needs analysis and to assist in the development of the program. An overview of the 1986 program is shown in Figure 6–3.

The program, called "Exploring Global Business Opportunities: Focus on Asia," was extremely ambitious. Its four objectives were:

- To learn a process for exploring foreign business opportunities and to apply the methodology to the Asian countries of highest interest to Emhart
- To determine the actions required for further enhancing Emhart's position in Asia
- To encourage sharing among participants by strengthening working relationships and teamwork
- To assist in continuing the transition to being a successful global competitor

To tackle that challenging list of objectives, Emhart enlisted the help of an impressive faculty that included scholars, consultants, and businesspeople with sound experience in Asia.

The 5½-day seminar conducted in 1986 began with a session, led by an expert in the field, devoted to examining Asia's role in the world economy. Quoting John Hay, secretary of state at the turn of the century, he told the Emhart executives that "the Mediterranean is the ocean of the past, the Atlantic is the ocean of the present, and the Pacific is the ocean of the future." John Hay's prediction is fast becoming a reality, the expert said, and then backed up that assertion with irrefutable evidence.

Figure 6–3. Emhart 1986 Executive Education Program, "Exploring Global Business Opportunities: Focus on Asia"—Overview.

ORIGINAL (1985) OVERALL NEEDS	PROGRAM CONCEPT	PROGRAM OBJECTIVES	SUBJECT MATTER

• To broaden and strengthen Emhart key management resources
 	
• To provide a continuing forum for management interchange and the exchange of ideas/experiences to build working relationships and foster teamwork
 	
• To review and reinforce the knowledge and skills required for success
	• A 5½-day Executive Education Program to provide:
	  – The practical competencies necessary to successfully explore business opportunities in the world marketplace
	  – A global business perspective essential to success in a world business environment
	
	• A program design which requires:
	  – The interchange of ideas and information among executives
	  – Cross-divisional/functional cooperation and coordination
	  – The application of new competencies to the development of individual and business action plans
		• Provide a "methodology" for exploring business opportunities in foreign countries: market, manufacturing/sourcing and competitive factors
		
		• Apply the "methodology" to Asian countries of special interest to Emhart
		
		• Assist Emhart in continuing the transition from a successful domestic company to a successful global competitor
		
		• Encourage the development of a global perspective in managing Emhart and each business unit
		
		• Provide a continuing forum for management interchange, building working relationships across divisions, establishing networks, sharing experiences and developing teamwork
			• Review of global competitiveness concepts from the 1985 program
			
			• Role and importance of the Asia marketplace
			
			• Business opportunity analysis process and framework
			
			• Exploring business opportunities in:
			  – China
			  – S. Korea
			  – Japan
			  – India
			  – Taiwan
			  – Thailand
			  – Indonesia
			
			• Cultural Differences
			
			• Strategic/portfolio view of Asia
			
			• Conclusions and Implications

As a fascinating two-hour panorama of the economies of Asia was presented by a consultant, the Emhart executives took notes at a feverish pace. With a wealth of data, the consultant took the group through the Pacific Basin country by country. A sampler of his remarks will illustrate why the Emhart executives were scribbling away:

> The bottom line, gentlemen, is this. After a decade of dramatic and unprecedented growth, the Pacific Basin countries are in trouble. Although the Thai economy is strong and the setback in Singapore appears to be temporary, with these exceptions the situation is problematic.
>
> The situation in Indonesia is critical. Unless oil prices recover to $14–17 a barrel, there will be severe structural problems in the economy for the next five years. There is also rising unemployment. Currently, some two million people—most of them immigrants—are out of work. That number is likely to increase over the next several years.
>
> Malaysia is in real trouble. The country has focused too much on heavy industry, causing structural problems in the economy that are likely to persist. The possibility of serious political difficulties also looms on the horizon.
>
> The Philippines is a mess. Government leadership is fragmented and inexperienced. Debt is enormous and rising, and the potential for a military coup is real. . . . Yet this environment creates new opportunities precisely because of the difficulties. There is an increasing emphasis on the private sector. Foreign investors are more welcome, particularly if they bring "appropriate" manufacturing with them.
>
> My advice? There are some opportunities, but choose your investments wisely. In other words, do exactly what you would do in any other part of the world: look before you leap.

This session included a comparative analysis of economic and political trends in the Asian countries, as well as of Asia compared to the United States, Europe, and Latin America. It also included an assessment of the major factors contributing to the growing importance of Asia.

With the appetites of the Emhart executives sufficiently whetted, the discussion then turned to the topic, "Exploring Global Business Opportunities." The discussion was led by professors from the University of Michigan and the Harvard Business School who had developed a methodology, specifically designed for Emhart, for exploring global business opportunities. The objective of the session was to define and apply the features of an effective process for exploring business opportunities in foreign countries.

To illustrate how the methodology can be applied in the real world, and bowing to its sheer size, the People's Republic of China was examined first. A professor from the University of Michigan's Center for China Studies and a retired president of AMF International teamed up to present a stimulating and insightful view of business opportunities—as well as pitfalls—in China.

Although it is impossible to do justice here to the scope and intelligence of the presentation, a few pearls will give the reader some indication of what the Emhart executives learned that day:

- The most valuable commodity the Western businessperson can bring to China is not goods, not services, not technology, and not currency. All these are important. But what is paramount are jobs.
- The business environment in China is incredibly bureaucratic. As an American, you will enter the system through a trading company. Before it can do anything, however, it needs the approval of several layers of the bureaucracy, including the Ministry of Electronics, for example, and then perhaps the People's Bank, the State Economic Commission, and the State Planning Commission. You need to understand that, and you need the services of someone who can move you through the web of approvals.
- Despite myths to the contrary, you can negotiate anything in China.
- Do a lot of homework on where you want to locate in China. Don't spread yourself too thin. Pick one area—whether it's Canton or Shanghai or Peking or the Manchurian Corridor—and take a rifle approach to it.
- You must go to China for the long haul. Get in with a small operation or venture, and then move slowly. But do so with a long-term strategy firmly in mind.

Equally valuable and powerful was a presentation by Jacques Maisonrouge, former head of IBM's World Trade Division. Maisonrouge focused his comments on the human resources side of becoming a global competitor. "To be successful in the world arena," he told his attentive audience, "the company must have clearly articulated ethical standards that are understood by all employees worldwide; short- and long-term objectives that are well defined and precise; and a burning dissatisfaction with the status quo."

With regard to the management team needed to be a successful global competitor, Maisonrouge stressed four attributes:

First, you must have a broad knowledge of the world at the senior corporate level. Second, you must have people who understand the way each country you intend to do business in operates—its power structure, its economic system, its legislative process. Third, you must have a cadre of business managers who understand cultural differences and are comfortable living with them, men and women who can *listen* to people of other cultures and *respect* their viewpoint. And fourth, you must have senior people who have worked in a variety of foreign cultures.

This type of practical, hard-hitting advice was a hallmark of the Emhart program. Said one participant: "I'm not sure what I expected, but I didn't expect this. We got a superb methodology for assessing our opportunities in a foreign country and then the opportunity to use that methodology under the auspices of academics and businessmen who knew what they were talking about. It exceeded my wildest expectations."

Following China, the program provided similar analyses of Japan, India, and South Korea. Finally, seminar participants applied the methodology to the "elective" country of greatest interest to them: Taiwan, Thailand, or Indonesia.

Emhart's 1986 Executive Education Program ended by having the executives grapple with what they had learned and apply it to Emhart. As in the original session of the program, they first identified personal insights and developed individual action plans for their area of responsibility. Then they were broken up into subgroups to "brainstorm" a list of the issues they felt needed to be addressed in order to strengthen Emhart's effectiveness as a total enterprise in Asia. After reaching consensus on the two or three issues that were most critical to Emhart's success, each group then prepared a 15-minute presentation that included the following:

- A brief description of the nature of each issue, problem, or opportunity
- The group's assessment of the impact of solving the problem, seizing the opportunity, or addressing the issue
- A recommended list of specific actions that Emhart might take to effectively deal with the issue

On Saturday morning—the culmination of the week-long seminar—the subgroups presented their recommendations to one of Emhart's top three executives; either Emhart's new chairman, Peter Scott, Vice Chairman Ruffi, or CEO William Lichtenfels. These three laid particular stress on the seriousness of the presentations. Ruffi reminded the participants that the recommendations they had made at the previous seminar resulted in "significant and substantial changes in our corporate mission statement, in our Far East strategy, in our intercompany pricing policy, in our management of technology, and in our sourcing of materials and parts. We intend to take your recommendations here this morning equally seriously. You will be kept informed of the actions we take as a result of your presentation."

Scott and Lichtenfels had similar messages. Lichtenfels told the group he participated in that "you have been heard, loud and clear. We will digest your recommendations, put them side by side with those of the other groups, and let you know where they lead us. I can assure you there will be action."

All told, the three executives heard a dozen presentations on what Emhart should do to become a more effective global competitor. If there was any one common denominator in the presentations, it was that they were uniformly constructive, reasoned, and sound. A synopsis of one, "Four Action Items Aimed at Expanding Emhart's Presence in Asia," is reprinted as the appendix to this chapter.

According to Lichtenfels, "We took these recommendations very, very seriously. Some were implemented. Some were studied and found to be not workable for one reason or another. Others are still being honed with an eye toward eventual implementation. None were summarily discarded."

One of the clear successes of Emhart's Executive Education Program was the expansion of its Hong Kong office. As a direct result of several similar recommendations, Emhart substantially expanded its sourcing capabilities in the Pacific Basin. Following the seminars, a corporate task force was set up to investigate the level and types of sourcing the company's operating unit was involved in throughout the Pacific Basic area.

The task force found that 17 percent of the materials used by Emhart annually was purchased in the region. That amounted to some $130 million a year. To bring more order to this purchasing, says Director of Corporate Purchasing Wally Werner, it is now being coordinated by Emhart's eight-person Hong Kong office.

Werner predicts that within a couple of years up to $20 million worth of materials will be purchased in the region on behalf of Emhart units in other parts of the world. "We should get significant savings on those materials," he says. "We're looking for at least 25 percent immediately and expect an eventual average of 50 percent."

Werner also believes that the purchase of materials from Mainland China will help promote expanded sales and marketing efforts there. "Our ability to sell in China is sometimes limited by that country's shortage of foreign capital," he says. "That situation would change if we purchase their goods. . . . This kind of arrangement would not only give us lower cost materials, but can open the door for us in one of the most significant growth areas in the world today."

Ambitious as these results of the Executive Education Program are, they are only the tip of the iceberg. "The real benefits are the intangible ones," says Lichtenfels.

> Our executives came away with a more realistic view of what it takes to be successful worldwide. Some of our shoe people used to salivate at the thought of penetrating the Chinese market, for instance. They talked about the billion people in China and talked, as shoe people do, about the two billion feet in China. During the course, they came to the realization that the economy is still way underdeveloped and that, at most, there are a hundred million consumers in China.
>
> They also learned that doing business in China and in many other countries takes time and that you have to choose your opportunities carefully.
>
> The program—both programs really—accomplished what we wanted. It helped us think globally. It got all of us on the same wavelength. It gave us an appreciation for both the risks and the benefits. It was a good investment.

Adds Ford: "No question it was a good investment. That's because we knew what we wanted. It wasn't training for training's sake. It had a purpose and solved a real need."

Postscript: The top management team at Emhart has changed since this chapter was initially prepared for publication. The company's new leadership elected to curtail the emphasis on executive education and to let the managers in each division determine the education needed to expand in global markets. The decision demonstrates the importance of top management support for executive education. Executive education will not—indeed cannot—flourish without the continued commitment of the CEO. When the CEO at Emhart believed that executive education could help him go global, it blossomed; when the new CEO did not share that vision, the program withered and eventually died.

APPENDIX: FOUR ACTIONS AIMED AT
EXPANDING EMHART'S PRESENCE IN ASIA

The six-person group began by identifying both the problems and the opportunities presented to Emhart by the proposition of expanding its business interests in Asia. The problems included the clear need for a different organization structure to do business in that part of the world; the need for a strong, long-term corporate commitment; the investment of both human and financial resources; the need for an organization to do business in that part of the world; and the need for more intelligence and information on Asia.

But if the group saw problems in expanding Emhart's business in Asia, it also saw large opportunities. Many of the countries of Asia represent huge potential markets that are growing rapidly—more rapidly in most cases than the United States and Western Europe. Additionally, Asia offers Emhart the opportunity to seize a competitive edge, to preempt the competition, and to serve the company as an important sourcing platform.

The group concluded that the opportunities far outweighed the problems and that Emhart should begin immediately to seriously plan for major, long-term expansion into Asia. This will have a tremendous impact on the corporation. It will entail a new organization; new approaches to doing business in new and vastly different cultures; and a financial investment that includes "people as well as bricks and mortar and which it is too early to identify and quantify."

Four specific actions were recommended to begin to move Emhart forward in Asia.

First, the corporation should develop a strong corporate statement on its intentions, its objectives and its commitments in Asia, including the level of resources it intends to invest and the time schedule for these investments. Although most groups identify opportunities for themselves and pursue business opportunities within their own units, this group felt strongly that the corporate commitment and direction needed to be articulated in a formal corporate statement.

Second, each group should develop its own plan for doing business in Asia. This plan should follow the model used during the week's discussion and should include a detailed country analysis; identification of the key opportunities for the group in each country in which it plans to begin or expand its operations; a statement of its strategic mission; a description of the management approach it will take; and a competitive analysis.

Third, at the same time the group plans are being developed, *an overall corporate action plan should also be developed.* Examples of the kinds of issues that should be included in the corporate plan include:

- A plan to establish and/or expand the corporate identity in Asia in general, and in key countries in particular
- A plan to develop the human resources needed to do business in Asia, including human resource policies and plans to develop and people
- A plan to facilitate the gathering and exchange of business information, intelligence, and experience among groups
- An examination and possible modification of Emhart's business policies to take into account new cultures and new government structures

Fourth, the group and corporate plans should be coordinated and integrated into one overall plan. This will provide consistency and synergy; will enable Emhart to leverage what it already is doing in Asia; will set clear priorities for the entire corporation; will allow Emhart to use its resources more effectively; and will generally increase Emhart's corporate competence in Asia.

IV DEREGULATION

7 DEVELOPING EXECUTIVE TALENT AT NORTHERN TELECOM

Northern Telecom Limited is Canada's largest supplier of equipment for integrated telecommunications networks. It is the second largest, after American Telephone & Telegraph, in the United States, and the fourth largest worldwide. The company traces its history back nearly a century, when it was created as a manufacturing division of Bell Canada.

In the 1970s, the company became a telecommunications giant. In 1976, in fact, Northern Telecom was the first company to publicly underwrite the production of a complete family of products and systems based on digital technology. At the time it was quite a risk, but one that has since paid off handsomely. The new product line, dubbed the Digital World Program, has since been copied by every major telecommunications manufacturer in the world.

Today, Northern Telecom's products and systems are marketed in some 90 countries. They are used not only by telephone operating companies but in business, government, educational, health, and military organizations. These products run the gamut of telecommunications equipment and include switching and transmission systems, data communications systems, wire and cable, business communications systems, terminals, and other equipment for a dazzling variety of public and private networks and systems.

The U.S. subsidiary—Northern Telecom, Inc. (NTI), of Nashville, Tennessee—was born out of the deregulation of the telephone industry in the early 1970s. The Bell System, which had grown up in a monopolistic marketplace, was slow to react to its new competitive environment. Innovation and risk-taking were not exactly hallmarks of the culture found in what, under deregulation, had become the Bell Operating Companies.

Yet taking risks and being innovative were precisely the qualities needed to seize and maintain a competitive edge in the newly deregulated telecommunications industry. A vacuum of sorts had been created, and Northern Telecom quickly stepped in.

Central to its strategy was the establishment of Northern Telecom Inc. (NTI) as its U.S. operating company in 1972. Rapid growth and a series of acquisitions followed, and today NTI employs more than 22,000 people and operates 14 manufacturing plants, an additional 13 research and development facilities, and more than 100 sales and service centers across the United States.

Desmond Hudson became Northern Telecom's president from a previous position as Group Vice President, Business Communications Systems, Northern Telecom, Dallas. His mission: to mine the riches and opportunities created by deregulation of the telephone industry.

PLENTY OF GROWTH, BUT
TOO LITTLE DIRECTION

The company Hudson inherited was far from ideal. In fact, it was in serious trouble. It was growing rapidly, but losing money. It had enormous potential, but little strategy to exploit it. It had good people, but little direction. Des Hudson recalls those early days vividly.

> When I arrived in Nashville in 1982, I found a company that was doing all it could to merely respond to enormous business opportunities. Because of the market's volatility, there was little agreement on where we were going and how we were going to get there. There was no agreement on how we were going to manage the business because the rules of the game seemed to change every time we turned around. In fact, we had different business units going off in different directions. In some cases, they were even competing with one another.

Despite the problems of trying to maintain control and develop direction in a turbulent industry, Hudson knew he had inherited a group of good people. They came from different companies with different cultures and different values, and Hudson knew right away that he had to develop a method of communicating Northern Telecom's values and culture to this diverse group.

"The thing that struck me almost immediately," says Hudson, "was that somehow I had to get through to a lot of people—to all the people really—and that somehow I had to do that quickly. But even before that we had to develop answers to some pretty fundamental questions. Who are we? What was our business? How were we going to cooperate and build teamwork? What was our sense of identity and strategic direction?"

Hudson brought his general managers together and began listening to them. They confirmed his worst fears: the corporation lacked a common vision and a shared set of core values. He then brought in the human resource people to help decide what steps Northern Telecom needed to take. The human resource staff wrote a manual for general managers, reissued Northern Telecom's policy guide, and began to determine what training was needed.

"The most frustrating thing we found," says Hudson, "was that we had some very bright people who were managers but needed more training in the basics of planning, organizing, and controlling. So we needed a process to get the fundamentals of management in place and then a process to develop and communicate a consensus on how we wanted to manage within the Northern Telecom framework."

DISCOVERING THE BUILDING BLOCKS APPROACH

Before going any further, Northern Telecom got input from the managers themselves through a series of interviews. Out of those interviews came several important messages:

1. It became clear that a systematic, centralized management development process was needed to integrate organizational and group goals.
2. Centralized management training should serve as an umbrella and provide common linkage, consistency, and compatibility among the divisions.
3. The individual manager is the fundamental element—the raison d'etre—of training.

According to Hudson:

> Those three findings led us to the development of something we call the "building blocks" approach to training . . . It lets us concentrate on the individual manager and what he or she needs to be effective. A hidden benefit—and a really powerful one for the Northern Telecom I found in 1982—is the enormous potential the building block approach provides for networking and team-building. For some people it's the first chance they've had to spend some serious time with people in other areas of the business.

A word is in order to explain what is meant by the term *building blocks*. Simply put, the building block approach to management development uses core, mandatory training programs—or blocks—that follow a sequential order and "build" on one another. This approach rests on the assumption that there are certain critical points in a manager's career when the challenges are new and developing the knowledge and skills required to meet them can't be left to chance. Consequently, each block addresses the very different skills and needs of managers at different points in their careers.

There are typically three blocks:

1. The first block of training is given as an individual assumes his or her first management assignment.
2. The second block is given when the individual becomes a middle manager, who is usually defined as a person who manages people who manage others.
3. The third block is given when an individual moves into senior management—an assignment that involves, for example, developing strategy and policy or managing multiple functions or businesses.

The building block approach has the strength of a pyramid—building upon and reinforcing itself and allowing managers to expand on and add to their existing abilities in a logical progression. When properly designed—that is, when tailored to specific company goals while at the same time developing the whole individual—each succeeding block builds upon the former. It is a permanent and continuing method for grooming executives and giving them increased levels of skills and knowledge.

A very powerful by-product of the building block approach is the opportunity for senior management of the corporation to build and reinforce corporate values, management philosophy and practices, and corporate culture at points in an individual's career that are "rites of passage." As the manager moves into each successive layer of management, he or she is put in touch with the corporation's core beliefs. The blocks are usually designed and developed centrally to ensure consistent high quality and to avoid overlap between the training developed at head-quarters and that done in divisions at NTI.

The building block approach has many benefits:

- It demonstrates a corporation's commitment to employee development.
- It helps shape and promulgate the corporate culture.
- It minimizes the chance for management mistakes and errors due to lack of the knowledge or skills that are taught in the training blocks.
- It ensures the cost-effective delivery of consistent, high quality, professional training.
- It provides the foundation for decentralization in that it develops a cadre of managers who can manage "decentrally" because they have the core skills and knowledge required, yet they adhere to a common set of values and principles.
- It provides an attractive tool for recruitment of new managers and the retention of those already on board because it demonstrates a commitment to their development.

Perhaps some or all of these benefits were on Hudson's mind as he formulated plans for NTI's management training program. In an effort to emphasize training and to make the building block concept a reality, Hudson and his top-management team took three specific actions. They held a General Managers' Conference in early 1984; they established a Northern Telecom management development center in Nashville; and they authorized the development of the Building Blocks Program.

At the General Managers' Conference, the top 60 GMs were told of the importance of management development and their responsibility to invest time and resources in the development of their people. "In the next few years," they were told by Gary Donahee, vice-president of human resources at Northern Telecom, "professionalism and productivity will be key to Northern Telecom's continued rapid growth as the world's leading supplier of fully digital telecommunications systems.

The question then becomes, what can be done to support the growing professionalism and productivity of our managerial resources? Certainly not the whole answer, but definitely a major component, is managerial training."

Des Hudson was quite clear on what he expected to accomplish:

> I expected the program to enhance the effectiveness and performance of the general managers and to help establish a foundation of skills the general manager needed to do his or her job. I wanted to expose the general managers to state-of-the-art management tools and processes in order to increase their effectiveness. I wanted to increase their knowledge of and commitment to our strategy, our direction, and our culture. And I wanted to build teamwork and cooperation.

To back these words up with actions, Northern Telecom established a world-class Management Development Center (MDC) in Nashville. In a brochure that received broad distribution in the company, Hudson emphasized the importance of the center and explained why manager participation in MDC programs would be mandatory: "[1] Managers too often find it necessary to put off personal and professional development for a more convenient time—which may never come. This quickly leads to obsolescence and stagnation in today's changeable world; and [2] We believe the health and continued growth of Northern Telecom depends on the acquisition, management, and development of competent human resources."

Mandatory training was a key concept of the Management Development Center. "At certain times in your Northern Telecom career," Hudson told one group of managers, "you will be asked to go to a center-sponsored training experience. It's an invitation you really can't turn down." The Management Development Center had five objectives:

1. To reinforce the common understanding of the way managers manage and interact with their employees, their customers, and their communities
2. To provide consistent, high-quality programs for all managers
3. To maximize overall training and development effectiveness, efficiency, and continuity
4. To meet current and future plans
5. To define, shape, and promote a Northern Telecom management culture

THE BUILDING BLOCKS PROGRAM

If Hudson's brochure sent a strong message of management commitment and supplied the bricks and mortar, then the Building Blocks Program provided the meat and potatoes. As with most building block approaches, Northern Telecom's has three training blocks—one for new managers, one for middle managers, and one for senior and/or general managers. The rationale and objectives for each of the three blocks are shown in Figure 7–1.

Building Block I

The new-manager block is based on the assumption that all new managers should learn Northern Telecom management philosophy and policies, as well as the knowledge and skills they need to do their jobs, as soon as possible after they are appointed. Consequently, the new-manager block:

- indoctrinates participants in Northern Telecom management philosophy, values, and culture;
- defines the role and responsibilities of first-line management;
- provides common knowledge and skills in the fundamentals of management;
- builds teamwork; and
- helps participants gain an understanding of the total Northern Telecom organization.

Building Block II

All participants in the second-stage, middle-management block must first have mastered the unique knowledge and skills associated with the first-stage, new-manager block sometime prior to promotion to middle management.

The middle-management block is intended to:

- communicate, build, and expand the manager's understanding of Northern Telecom's philosophy and culture;
- define the roles and responsibilities of the middle manager;

Figure 7–1.   Northern Telecom Building Blocks Program.

NEW MANAGER BLOCK

Rationale
All managers new to management at Northern Telecom should learn the Northern Telecom management philosophy/policies and required knowledge/skills as soon as possible after appointment.

Objectives
- Indoctrinate in NT management philosophy/values (culture)
- Define role/responsibilities of first line manager
- Provide common knowledge/skills in fundamentals of management
- Build teamwork
- Gain understanding of total Northern Telecom organization

MIDDLE MANAGER BLOCK

Rationale
All new middle managers (e.g., manage other managers) should learn the unique knowledge/skills required to successfully manage and be able to reinforce the concepts of the New Manager Block.

Objectives
- Communicate and build NT management philosophy/values (culture)
- Define role/responsibilities of middle manager
- Provide common knowledge/skills in managing managers
- Build teamwork

SENIOR MANAGEMENT BLOCK

Rationale
All new senior managers should learn the knowledges/skills unique to the position (e.g., policy/strategy) and must reinforce the concepts of the new manager and Middle Manager Block.

Objectives
- Communicate and build NT management philosophy/values (culture)
- Define role/responsibilities of senior managers
- Provide common knowledge/skills required for effective senior managers
- Build teamwork
- Provide forum for communication and dialogue among participants as well as management
- Communicate and achieve participant understanding of NT strategic issues

- provide common knowledge and skills in managing managers; and
- build teamwork.

Building Block III

The third training block—the one for senior and general managers—
provides all participants with a refresher look at the first two blocks,
as well as with skills and knowledge aimed at satisfying the unique needs
of NTI's most senior executives. These include the need to understand
the company's broad strategic directions, the nature of Northern
Telecom's markets, the strengths and weaknesses of the competition,
and so on.

NTI's handling of the third training block was unique and is well
worth describing at some length. The traditional—and normally quite
appropriate—method of design and implementation is to begin with
the first block, the one designed for first-line managers. Once that process is up and running well, then the second block is added, and so
on until all three blocks are in place.

But these were not normal times for NTI, and therein lay a dilemma
for Hudson. If he stuck with the traditional approach, NTI's cadre of
senior managers would probably not be touched by the Building Blocks
Program for several years. During that period, the massive shakeouts
and explosive growth in the U.S. telecommunications industry that had
resulted from deregulation would undoubtedly continue. Hudson was
faced with a fairly narrow window of opportunity, on the one hand;
on the other, he was working with a senior management team that was
largely new, had been drawn from a variety of backgrounds and cultures,
and had varying degrees of knowledge, understanding, and commitment to the management style and strategic direction of Northern
Telecom Inc.

In a nutshell, Hudson faced this dilemma: enormous market and
strategic opportunities brought about by deregulations, and a senior
management team that needed a common vision and a set of core values
to maximize its advantage in the marketplace. Hudson recalls,

> When I took over Northern Telecom [NTI] I found a talented management
> team, but one that needed a more focused vision of where we wanted to be
> headed in the long-term. We also had no identifiable corporate culture because
> of the explosive growth in our industry and the time and energy required of a
> small organization to meet those challenges and opportunities. To succeed in

the marketplace, we had to respond to short-term demands. People just didn't have the time to begin thinking long term. But our long-term success depended on common vision and core values.

Hudson had four objectives for the Building Block III program:

- To review and reinforce the knowledge and skills required for effective management of the critical and current issues facing general managers
- To identify the culture of Northern Telecom Inc. and build management's philosophy, values, and style
- To provide a continuing forum for management interchange, to build working relationships across organizations, to establish networks, to share experiences, and to develop teamwork
- To review state-of-the-art business management concepts as they were being developed and applied in successful companies

That's a pretty tall order. To accomplish it, the professional executive development staff requested two full weeks of training. Hudson quickly granted the request. Under the general theme of "managing growth and change," Building Block III is in two parts: Week One focuses externally on building a market and customer orientation, and the second week looks internally at the general manager's role in managing the business.

Each week was designed to reinforce the basic core values of NTI managers: their commitment to their customers, their commitment to their people, their commitment to do what they say they will do for their customers, for each other, and for their employees.

The initial expectation for Building Block III was that the general managers would receive tools and techniques that they could use on the job to successfully confront the problems that existed in the telecommunications industry. Donahee explained that "what we didn't want was ethereal thinking. Our number-one objective was that the program be pragmatic, not academic, in nature and that the learning could be readily utilized back home."

Week one. The first week was intended to help the general managers better understand the market segments that Northern Telecom was in, the strategic significance of being there, and the competitive process shaping that market. Figure 7–2 provides an overview of the first week's schedule.

Figure 7-2. Northern Telecom Building Block #3, Week One: Building a Market and Customer Orientation.

	SUNDAY	MONDAY	TUESDAY	WEDNESDAY	THURSDAY	FRIDAY
Morning		• Building Competitive Advantage – Industry Analysis	• Building Competitive Advantage (Cont.) – Competitor Analysis	• Customer Satisfaction Panel Debriefing • Marketing Strategy	• Major Account Management	• Building A Market & Customer Orientation Workshop (Cont.) • Adjourn
		LUNCH	LUNCH	LUNCH	LUNCH	LUNCH
Afternoon	• Program Introduction	• Building Competitive Advantage (Cont.)	• Building Competitive Advantage (Cont.) – Action Planning • Customer Satisfaction Panel	• Service Strategy	• Value Added Marketing & Customer Service • Building A Market & Customer Orientation Workshop	
	DINNER	DINNER	DINNER	DINNER	DINNER	
Evening					• Building A Market & Customer Orientation Workshop (Cont.)	

As a prerequisite, the participants read a comprehensive industry paper that thoroughly described Northern Telecom competitors, its customers and suppliers, the prevailing barriers to entry into the industry, and substitutes in the telecommunications and management information systems industries. This paper formed the framework for in-class discussions on the markets and industries and Northern Telecom presence in those markets.

The first week was kicked off with a 1½-day session, "Building Competitive Advantage—Competitive Forces in the Industry," which was intended to help the general managers strengthen their strategic analysis skills through understanding and applying an industry analysis model. The model—developed by Michael Porter of Harvard University—had been sent ahead with the program prereading. The participants applied Porter's concepts and analytic tools in organizing and evaluating the information provided in the industry paper. In the process, strategic thinking skills emerged and a list of critical success factors was compiled. These factors were determined to be the key strategies and characteristics of the most successful companies in these industries. Having done this exercise, the participants examine Northern Telecom's relative position in its businesses, assess its chance for success, and identify areas in need of improvement and strengthening.

This was followed by a session on improving Northern Telecom's competitive position. The participants assessed Northern Telecom's relative position against its principal competitors currently, as well as in the future. They then analyzed and compared the forces at work in the industry and their competitive position against their current business strategies. For example, program participants were asked whether or not Northern Telecom's business strategies were properly aligned with the realities of the marketplace, the strengths and weaknesses of the competition, and the strengths and weaknesses of Northern Telecom itself.

Discussions and workshops then zeroed in on specific key competitors, including IBM and AT&T. In-depth analysis in team workshops enabled the participants to concisely describe the strengths, weaknesses, and principal strategies of their competitors. And then, on a macro level, the general managers—still in teams—explored Northern Telecom's current statements of its corporate strategies.

Finally, they evaluated the company's strategic position vis-a-vis its competitors. A half-day was devoted to this process, which allowed the participants, individually and collectively, to challenge the strategies of their own business units and to consider ways in which those strategies might be strengthened. During this session, a formalized action planning process encouraged the participants to formulate concrete ideas to improve their business unit's competitive position.

"For most of us," says one general manager who participated in the program, "this was the first opportunity we ever had to systematically examine the competition and analyze what it meant to us. A lot of us in this industry hadn't worried very much about competition. We were so regulated that we didn't have to pay a lot of attention to the competition. So this was all new and really focused a lot of heads on the new realities of the industry."

The general managers were also given the opportunity to focus on customers and to hear from them firsthand. This session provided an informal and candid forum for discussing the key issues existing between NTI and its customers. A no-holds-barred dialogue was encouraged. The overall guideline for the customers was that "anything on your mind is important for us to hear and understand." By listening to customer feedback on Northern Telecom's products, service, sales support, and administrative and systems support, the general managers were able to apply the information to developing new action plans and improving current methods for understanding the customer's requirements so as to ensure increased customer satisfaction in the future.

Because of the nature of their business, two major accounts were selected for each session. Typically, one was a Bell Operating Company and the other was an end-user. Participants chose which customer session to attend depending on their business unit and responsibilities.

Imagine it. Customers honestly assessing your strengths and weaknesses and, with that input, developing specific action plans to take back to your people. Controversial? Yes. Embarrassing? Certainly. Beneficial? You bet! In fact, Hudson still keeps a binder full of notes from the customer panels on his credenza because he finds different germs of ideas in it from time to time.

Hudson believes the customer panel was an excellent tool, "even if it hurt a little—even it it meant being judged." He explains that "the important thing is not to judge but to take the problem and hand it right to the person who should be fixing it, and judge only if the problem is not fixed."

Hudson and his senior staff did precisely that. Each problem that was identified was handed off to the appropriate person. Only in a few cases was it necessary to intercede and provide extra help and support. The results are difficult to quantify, but there is general agreement that they have been substantial. One participant put it this way: "It's an unbeatable combination. The participants are there to learn, so they're open-minded. The customers are encouraged to be open and forthright. The dialogue takes place at the training center, so the environment is right. A lot of us developed lasting relationships with key customers at those sessions. And all of us came away with a cleaner picture of what we had to do to improve customer satisfaction."

A hidden benefit of customer participation in Building Block III is the impact not only on NTI's general managers but on the customers themselves. "I'll be honest with you," said one large customer, "We were beginning to have some reservations about the company's commitment to us. Not after that seminar. We came away knowing that we could count on Northern Telecom to work with us. It was clear they they wanted to be part of the solution, not part of the problem."

After the session with customers, the next three dealt with marketing, service, and major account management. Each session was designed to provide the general managers with the necessary skills and knowledge to improve methods and results in each of these areas. A variety of outside experts presented leading-edge approaches and discussed successful practices in use at other top corporations. Learning came not just from the faculty, but from the participants themselves. They shared their own experiences, their successes and failures, their trials and errors. In the process of sharing, they learned from one another.

The session on major-account management was handled entirely by Northern Telecom executives. They outlined the company's policies, directions, and methods for dealing with large accounts. An emphasis was placed on understanding the role of the regional vice-president and how he or she interacts with customers, with product planning and design, and with operations and manufacturing. At the conclusion of this session, a workshop provided small groups of seminar participants with the opportunity to "teach each other," to share experiences, and to exchange ideas for self-improvement in dealing with the needs and requirements of major accounts.

Toward the end of the first week, time was spent reviewing the week's objectives, the important lessons that emerged, and the personal planning that had resulted. In the week's final workshop, participants divided up into groups by business unit, identified key issues facing them, as well as issues facing the company in building market and customer orientation. They then developed plans of action that were conveyed to the other participants and to a senior management panel. The role of the panel was to receive and respond to the proposals by clarifying the issues and action steps and by providing information and insights that would be beneficial in accomplishing the recommended actions. Hudson himself led the senior management panel.

But the presentations were not an end in themselves. They were geared toward action. Participants in the seminar developed *personal* action plans based on what they had learned about themselves and their company. They were encouraged to share their plans with two other people.

This sharing served two useful purposes. First, it gave participants the opportunity to have a few other people challenge their personal action plans, tell them what would help and what would not, and offer suggestions for additional actions to consider for improving leadership skills. And second, it committed each person to follow through on his or her action plan. It was no longer a mere sheet of paper that the general manager could choose to ignore back on the job. Now it was a plan that at least two peers knew about.

Said one participant: "Let's face it. You were hooked. And just to sink the hook a little deeper, you were told that during the second week of training, you would be asked to make a progress report. That did it for most of us. We left committed to implementing these action plans."

Week Two. So ended the first week of Building Block III. After six months of putting their new skills to work on becoming more market-driven and customer-oriented, the executives returned to the Management Development Center for the second half of their training. This second week, "Managing the Business—the GM Role," focused on strengthening the Northern Telecom Inc. culture and management style, as well as on improving the personal leadership style and skills of each participant. Figure 7–3 provides an overview of the second week.

The week started with an examination of both NTI's current culture and its desired culture, that is, its management values, philosophy, style, and practices. Understanding how the "NTI way" might differ among groups, the general managers learned how important it was to develop, strengthen, maintain, and communicate their experience of Northern Telecom Inc.'s culture.

To fully understand and characterize the current, as well as the desired, corporate culture, seminar participants participated in individual work, then in subgroup work, and finally in full-group work. In a sense, they created the culture, starting with the individual needs and perceptions of each participant and building to a consensus of the entire group.

Figure 7-3. Northern Telecom Building Block #3, Week Two: Managing the Business—The General Manager's Role.

MONDAY	TUESDAY	WEDNESDAY	THURSDAY	FRIDAY
• Welcome/ Introduction • Corporate Culture	• Human Resource Management	• Organizational Structure Issues in a Matrix Organization	• Business Simulation	• Conclusions/ Implications • Discussion with Senior Management • Adjourn
LUNCH	LUNCH	LUNCH	LUNCH	LUNCH
• Leadership Practices	• Organization Effectiveness and Change	• Financial Management	• Business Simulation (Cont.)	
DINNER	DINNER	DINNER	DINNER	
	• Work in Teams on Progress on Action Plans from the End of Week One		• Individual Action Planning	

A key part of this second week was the personal feedback that each participant received on his or her own leadership and management strengths and weaknesses. Here's how it worked.

Prior to Building Block III, it was determined that the general managers needed to better understand their own management styles and, based on feedback from subordinates, to identify ways of strengthening their management skills—especially through coaching and counseling. Consequently, prior to the program, a questionnaire on leadership practices had been sent to designated subordinates of each general manager. After they were completed, the questionnaires were processed and a confidential report was prepared and distributed at the program. The results reported each general manager's score in relation to all general managers at Northern Telecom Inc., as well as in relation to national norms. Individual coaching and counseling was available to the participants to help them interpret the meaning of their individual scores and to provide assistance in identifying appropriate actions they could take back on the job.

"This feature of the program," says one participant,

> was worth the price of admission alone. There's no doubt in my mind that it has helped me become a better manager. I'll give you just one example. I *thought* that I was a very participative manager and that I gave my people a lot of authority and responsibility to do things on their own. They had a different view. To them, I couldn't or wouldn't make decisions. That blew me away. But I promosed myself I would address the issue head-on. At my first staff meeting after the seminar, I raised the issue and we had a good discussion. I think their percpetion of me has changed for the better, and I know my behavior has changed.

Another feature of the second week was the emphasis on human resource management. With the rapid growth and change that Northern Telecom was experiencing, it was critical to help the general managers increase their effectiveness in attracting, maintaining, and retaining high-quality people. The session on human resource management was therefore designed to provide an understanding of several critical issues: the general manager's role in helping newly appointed managers survive, identifying and developing management talent, and recruiting, developing, retaining sales and technical people. Participants studied a case specific to NTI, shared their own experiences, and focused on the current policies and practices in addressing these issues. The discussions in this session led into the next session, wherein participants studied planning and managing organizational change and the critical success factors for managing in an environment of rapid internal growth and change.

After a comprehensive review of financial management terms and concepts, the general managers participated in a day-long, customized business simulation to integrate the key lessons from the entire program. Managed via personal computers, the simulation involved a series of business scenarios reflecting the real-world strategic and operating problems at the business unit level. During this structured, high-energy learning event, participants practiced and integrated what they had learned from all parts of Building Block III.

The simulation created an interactive, realistic, and demanding decisionmaking environment that encouraged a teamwork approach to solving complex business and organizational issues. At the beginning of the simulation, participants agreed on the "scoring" of the simulation results so that some of the critical behaviors central to the Northern Telecom Inc. culture would be reinforced.

At week's end, the participants were given the opportunity to translate what they had learned in both weeks of the program into specific action plans to be implemented when they returned to their offices. They were asked to:

- meet in the same subgroups they had formed in the first week of training;
- review the progress they had made since the first week;
- agree on additional actions required to complete the work and the due dates; and
- prepare a presentation for Hudson and his management team.

The results of these workshops were presented to Hudson and the group vice-presidents on the final day. Hudson thoroughly supported this process. "In terms of getting into the real issues," he said, "I think it is very, very important that we have the top manager involved to hear the recommendations. The risk, if there is one, is that there would be a focus on top management's issues rather than the real ones. But I don't think that happened. I think those discussions were very candid. I know they were very useful."

Hudson credits these presentations with some very specific actions. For example, NTI stopped paying commissions on sales to major accounts. Previously, there had been no incentive for one division to sell the products of another division; in fact, the rewards system actually contributed to a sense of competition among groups and divisions. Criticism of this situation came up repeatedly during the presentations, so Hudson directed that it be changed. The major accounts organization is now a noncommission organization, and there are new incentives to sell the total Northern Telecom Inc. product line.

Says Hudson:

> We also made some organization changes to focus our marketing efforts on the customer, the end-user. And there have been subtle changes as well, especially some that resulted from the customer feedback sessions. Because they're subtle, they're hard to explain. But there has been a change in the management style of the general managers. I think our motivation, vision, core values, and teamwork have never been stronger than they are today.

Hudson's original objective in launching Building Block III for general managers was to speed up their development. "That clearly happened," he says.

> We also arrived at a good consensus of precisely what the Northern Telecom [Inc.] way of managing was, what it meant. The second [benefit] was their understanding of the strategy and where we are heading. I couldn't do that by getting on an airplane, I couldn't do that by writing letters, although I tried a lot of standard techniques. So I was convinced the way it was going to get done was to get the general managers hearing the same message.

A WORTHWHILE INVESTMENT

We asked Hudson whether or not the investment in the Management Development Center and the Building Blocks Program has paid off. He replied,

> When I started talking about leasing space for a management training and development center and a building block program, I had to answer some tough questions about the financial investment. Businesses talk a lot about "our people," and how important they are, and about investing in "our people." But some companies are a little less committed when you start talking about money. But you have to invest and you've got to be in it for the long term. It's not a one-year shot. The payoff doesn't start showing up for eighteen to twenty-four months, but when it does, the payoff far exceeds the investment.

When asked about specific results, Hudson points out that overhead costs have been reduced by 50 percent in five years. "The whole organization is better focused. A focused organization can help you make financial targets. And we're making our targets. For any CEO, that's the bottom line."

Gary Donahee cites two factors in the success of the program. The first is that Northern Telecom took the time to do it right. "The last thing you want to do is put something in place that doesn't work," he explains. "You typically only get one crack at something like this. So we started out by looking at what other companies were doing and then testing that against the expectations and needs of our steering committee. We moved very deliberately."

The second factor that Donahee points to as being key to success is his "ace-in-the-hole": Hudson. "The Building Blocks don't belong to Gary Donahee," he says, "they belong to Des. From day one, he was the champion. He drove it and stuck behind it. There has never been a question of whether people were going to attend a program if they were invited or if we were going to cut back on the program. In that period, we have had to have moratorium on some training programs, but never on the Building Blocks Program."

Hudson has since been appointed president of Northern Telecom World Trade. One can't help but wonder what his plans for executive development are in his new assignment.

One last—but crucial—point. Decisions to create and implement a building blocks strategy almost always come from the very top of the corporation—from either a chief executive officer or a president who understands its importance. When Hudson was asked *why* he was the driver of Northern Telecom's Building Blocks Program, he seemd puzzled that the question was ever asked. Then the answer came. "Because," he said, "it's part of my job, part of my responsibility to the corporation and to my managers."

Roy Merrills replaced Des Hudson as NTI's president and is equally committed to executive development. Under Merrills' direction, plans are underway for Building Block #4 which will likely focus on leadership.

8 BELLSOUTH: SURVIVING AND EXCELLING AFTER DIVESTITURE

John Clendenin, chairman and chief executive officer of BellSouth, had much to be proud of as the corporation headed into the latter part of the 1980s. Always strong, BellSouth emerged from the storms of divestiture that drastically reshaped the U.S. telecommunications industry even stronger. Consider these facts:

- BellSouth became divested on January 1, 1984, with $21 billion in assets that have since grown to more than $28 billion.
- The company has remained the largest of the seven regional holding companies that were formerly part of AT&T.
- BellSouth now has more than 100,000 employees in forty-four states and fourteen countries.
- In recent rankings of America's largest companies by *Business Week* and *Forbes,* BellSouth placed seventh in market value, tenth in annual profits, and forty-seventh in annual sales.

BellSouth had the potential to emerge from the divestiture stronger and more dynamic than before and, in the process, to help change and shape the telecommunications industry forever. John Clendenin and his top management team had every intention to seize the opportunity as well as every reason to be optimistic. BellSouth inherited a rich tradition and sound financial underpinnings. It had been tested by, and

121

prospered under, the rigors of divestiture. Clendenin was certain the corporation would continue to carry on the excellent tradition of service earned under the AT&T umbrella.

Headquartered in Atlanta, Georgia, the BellSouth holding company includes South Central Bell, Southern Bell, BellSouth Services, and BellSouth Enterprises. South Central Bell and Southern Bell provide telecommunications and information distribution services to more than 15 million access lines in local exchange and exchange access markets in nine southeastern states. BellSouth Services provides centralized planning, information systems services, and administrative support functions for the telephone subsidiaries. BellSouth Enterprises operates nonlocal exchange services and operations in forty-four states and sixteen countries.

NEW LEADERSHIP NEEDS

By virtually any standard, BellSouth is a huge and successful enterprise. Yet there was reason for concern in January 1984 as it began its maiden voyage. Whereas it had once navigated in waters protected by both AT&T and government regulation, it was now to be tested in the unchartered waters of competition and the free market system.

Clendenin and his senior executives knew that if BellSouth was to make the adjustment from a heavily regulated to a deregulated environment, its managers would have to be empowered to act as leaders now more than ever. Deregulation and the opening of the industry to competition made it vital that decisions be made more quickly and forcefully. Leadership has become more critical.

How would BellSouth executives respond to the competitive challenge? What changes would they have to make? What new skills would they have to acquire? BellSouth managers had grown accustomed to competing internally, but would they be able to face external competition for the first time in the history of the industry?

"As our management grappled with these questions," said Clendenin, "we kept coming back to a single answer. We needed a world-class executive training and education capability designed specifically for our unique needs. Our vision was that this would begin with the very top of the house, myself included, and then spread to all our senior and middle managers."

The company paid little attention to executive development in the late 1970s and early 1980s, and for some legitimate reasons. According to Clendenin,

> We had been an extremely busy, dynamic company during that period. We had gone through a massive restructuring aimed at making us more of a market-driven company. We were preoccupied for a time with competitive and regulatory changes. Then divestiture totally consumed us. And for the two years immediately preceding the birth of BellSouth (1982–83), our financial performance was very good. So in that environment, executive development was something that had not received a lot of attention, and it was time to focus on it again. In fact, it was essential that we do so.

THE CREATION OF THE BELLSOUTH MANAGEMENT INSTITUTE

Clendenin and his top management team had several things in mind when they began to refocus on management and executive education. They wanted a "college of some kind," with a specific charter to develop a cadre of executives capable of leading BellSouth into the twenty-first century. They wanted a long-term process that would last a decade or more. They wanted the curriculum not only to teach but to motivate. And they wanted this internal development program, which would be targeted at the top 5 percent of BellSouth managers and executives, to be world-class.

The person chosen to take on the assignment elicited surprise. Some excellent human resource professionals were passed over. The idea of bringing in someone from the academic community was rejected. Instead, an engineer with limited executive development experience was chosen to direct management training and development and to create the BellSouth Management Institute: James D. Moore. One BellSouth executive close to the situation said that "the selection of Jim raised some eyebrows at the time, but in retrospect it could not have been a better choice. He brought no baggage with him—no preconceived ideas of what was needed or what wouldn't work. He started with a clean sheet of paper."

Moore's background included more than twenty years of service with the former Bell System, most of it in network operations management. His previous assignment was with Bell Communications Research, and his academic training included a master's degree in electrical engineering from the University of Louisville. As one of his biographies points out, tongue in cheek, "He brings to the job absolutely no prior experience in any human resource field." That is not quite true. Moore did have considerable experience in technical training—experience he calls "irrelevant" to executive education.

"When I arrived on the scene," says Moore, "I was immediately impressed by John Clendenin's support, and I became more and more convinced that he was committed and serious—very serious—about the role that executive education could play in ensuring BellSouth's continued leadership in a fast-moving and intensely competitive marketplace." Moore also knew that he had to seize the opportunity presented to him. "I hit the ground running," he says "and made some early decisions." In retrospect, those decisions were critical.

The first was not to hire a large staff of human resource professionals. "I wanted to approach executive education from a very different vantage point. You will notice that I never use the word *training*. I removed it from my vocabulary," says Moore. "That's because *training* implies that a trainer has a command of skill or knowledge he or she will impart to a group of students that do not have that same skill or knowledge. That concept, it seems to me, does not fit all cases when it comes to executive education. There is a need for greater discovery and involvement on the part of the executives."

Another reason Moore did not want to build up a large staff of human resource professionals had to do with credibility. "It seemed to me," he says, "that the human resource people—and ours are darned good—could not possibly have the credibility and the experience to actually teach our senior people. So I decided to rely heavily on outside experts—people with national and international reputations in some particular area we need."

A second critical decision Moore made early on had to do with the structure and delivery of executive education within BellSouth. There was some feeling that executive education should focus on building the strengths of tomorrow's executives—highly talented people in middle management who had been identified as being capable of moving into the executive ranks in the future. "For some companies," said Moore, "that would make a lot of sense. But not for us. We were attempting to transform the entire corporate culture and therefore needed the entire management team to participate. We also decided to start at the very top—literally, with the senior management team."

Consequently, BellSouth's executive education program initially targeted the top 1 percent of the corporate structure. BellSouth has some 30,000 managers. Initially, executive education focused on the top 300; eventually, the program was expanded to include 1200 people. "That strategy worked well," said Moore. "Middle managers wanted to attend the training because they saw early on that even senior executives were attending and benefiting from it. They realized that we were not trying to fix something that was broken. Rather, we were trying to strengthen an already strong management team."

Moore's third crucial decision had to do with content: he decided he was not in a position to determine it. He turned instead to the senior executives themselves and conducted a needs analysis, including in-depth interviews with the chief executive officer, the presidents, several senior corporate officers, and a few focus groups of other senior managers. Several major findings and issues emerged from this analysis. We will discuss the five most important.

First, the lack of a "future orientation" was creating uncertainty about BellSouth's ability to succeed in a highly competitive market. Executives had a clear understanding of their functional or divisional plans and strategies but felt the company's overall strategic direction had not been clearly interpreted and communicated. "That created ambivalence and a certain sense of fear," said one executive. "Some of us were saying that we knew what we were doing as individual organizations, but we couldn't be sure it fit with a strategy. We didn't really talk about it, but we were concerned whether we could make it big after divestiture."

Second, people at all levels—from upper-middle management to the service employees—seemed to be waiting to be told what to do. They had not been empowered to act and did not have the freedom needed to solve problems. Decisions were pushed further and further up the organization. Managers, of course, were part of the problem. They had learned their jobs in a culture that expected and encouraged the manager to manage tightly, to play the role of expert on all matters, to constantly check employee performance, and to personally make all the decisions and call all the shots. While this style of management served BellSouth well in the old regulated environment, it would not be as effective in the future. The new environment required that all employees have more power to act and that managers serve as facilitators and enablers.

Third, the credibility of senior management was *perceived* as "part of the problem." BellSouth employees seemed to realize that change was needed and even essential if the new company was to build on the solid performance and growth of the old, and they also seemed to realize that senior executives themselves had to take the lead. According to one manager, "People were saying to the senior team that they would change when the executives changed. There was also a line that was commonly used, that executives did not 'walk like they talk.' In other words, the corporate rhetoric and pronouncements said one thing, but [executives] acted [in] another."

Fourth, the newly issued corporate value statements were perceived as lacking enough substance to serve as operational guidelines. People did not quarrel with the values or the words, but they saw little connection between their daily work and corporate goals and strategies. There was also a perception of conflict between those values and the real world. One executive commented, "Mixed messages were being sent. On the one hand, we would say that the customer was all-important. On the other hand, we would cut costs and sometimes impact the level of service we could provide. You always have these trade-offs, of course, but our people did not understand them, and the values became words that had little meaning."

Fifth, many internal procedures, processes, and systems appeared to be out of alignment with the desired direction of BellSouth. The company wanted to be more adaptive, more responsive, and more flexible. Yet little or nothing had been put in place to make this happen. A synopsis of the needs analysis findings is presented in Figure 8–1.

These findings confirmed Clendenin's belief that BellSouth's executives were ready for help, according to Moore, "They were concerned about their own preparation to lead BellSouth into a new era."

Figure 8–1.   Issues Identified by Needs Analysis at BellSouth.

OLD CULTURE	DESIRED CULTURE
Little understanding of strategic direction	Clear understanding of and confidence in strategic direction
People not empowered to act	Highly participative environment
Manager as "expert"	Manager as "facilitator"
Executives "talking" right	Executives "walking" right
Value statements perceived as nice words only	Value statements perceived as operational guidelines
Conflict between stated objectives and organizational processes	Alignment between objectives and processes

A key word here is *preparation*. Neither Clendenin nor his top executive team were concerned about their abilities. After all, they had led the old company to its position as the largest and perhaps the most successful of AT&T's regional operating companies. But the rules were changing, and the ground beneath them was shifting. They were looking for ways to increase their effectiveness in preparing for the future.

The prescription was bold and sweeping. The BellSouth Management Institute was established, put in place quickly, and made a permanent part of the BellSouth landscape and culture. The direction given to Moore was powerful:

- Be a catalyst for change. Take a leadership role in reshaping the culture and adjusting the way BellSouth runs its business.
- Provide a forum for identifying what needs to change at BellSouth and for initiating action to bring about those changes.
- Be a part of the communication and commitment process. Help explain where BellSouth is heading, how it intends to get there, and what role each individual will play in forging the new direction.
- Shape attitudes and provide critical education. Provide the executive team with the skills, tools, and developmental experiences it needs to continue to succeed.
- Translate the needs of the business into education programs that are directly related to those needs and to the business strategy.
- Be different. Set an example for change. Be bold and imaginative. Take managers out of their comfort zone.

Moore felt that the design of the Management Institute programs had to be unique, innovative, and engaging. BellSouth was not only interested in informing executives and exposing them to new information and ideas, it also wanted to change behavior and have the institute programs model the desired behavior. For example, BellSouth wanted managers to be creative and innovative; the institute programs therefore needed to be innovative in the learning methods used.

The BellSouth Management Institute has become, in my experience, one of the best of its kind in the world.

It cannot be overemphasized that the BellSouth Management Institute is *not* a one-time program. It is in place for the long term. One admiring human resource professional in another company said, "This is a critical difference at BellSouth. They are clearly in this for the long haul. Most of us design a program, implement it, and then sit back and admire it. Not them. They have a game plan that goes on and on and an institutionalized corporate organization to support it."

This process approach to executive education is depicted in Figure 8–2. Although the actual implementation process has changed somewhat, that is not the point. The point is that there are a long-range plan and process in place and a commitment to executive education that is real and demonstrable.

It is also noteworthy that the BellSouth Management Institute provides support that goes beyond the courses it provides. It also houses an extensive library and a large collection of cassette tapes, audiovisual programs, and self-help books that cover leadership and management, business skills and trends, personal and professional success strategies, self-improvement, communications skills, inspiration and motivation, entrepreneurship and financial growth, and salesmanship.

Still another feature of the institute is the *Leadership Digest*. The first issue, published in 1987, describes its role:

> The role of our bimonthly newsletter is to reinforce the experiences that the Management Institute will offer top managers through its *Executive Leadership Series* programs. A free subscription will be sent to all managers in this group.
>
> Each issue concentrates on a *theme* relating to leadership in BellSouth. You'll get different perspectives on this theme from some of the greatest thinkers and achievers of today and yesterday. Each issue also provides you with the thoughts of a key BellSouth leader on the theme.
>
> The *Leader's Library* briefly reviews books, articles, or tapes that have special applicability to the issue's theme.
>
> There'll be information, humor, anecdotes, anything that we can think of to reinforce your changing leadership role.

Figure 8–2.   BellSouth Management Institute: Executive Leadership Series.

The needs analysis, Clendenin's own personal conviction, and the unique position that BellSouth found itself in all pointed in one direction: the institute should initially focus on leadership development. That's precisely what happened. The initial *Leadership Digest* includes this article to explain the rationale for the central theme of leadership.

Why We Need Education and Self-Development for Leadership

All of us want to be successful leaders and managers because our success benefits both us and the organizations for which we're responsible. All of us succeed much of the time, yet few of us examine how we personally affect the outcome.

Have our skills been outdated? Have we lost our sense of perspective? Are we uncomfortable with the inevitability of change? Do we understand our capabilities and limitations?

These are questions that our situations rarely force us to ask ourselves. It's easier to accept the success that we have achieved as proof that we're O.K. as is. Even if we should pose the questions, it's doubtful that we could answer them because few of us can see ourselves objectively.

Executive education and personal development courses force us to assess ourselves in relation to what's happening today, and what's likely to be happening tomorrow, in our jobs and our lives. They give us the tools to develop ourselves as managers and as leaders.

Management requires the skills that allow us to plan, organize, delegate, and analyze.

Leaders need a mindset, an approach to themselves, their jobs, their organizations—to life itself—that allows them to see not only the present situation, but also the possibilities of the future.

A few companies have begun to offer their *top managers* various kinds of *executive* education to reinforce the capabilities and the mindset needed for management and leadership. Some executive education focuses on the updating and enhancing of specific managerial skills. Other approaches concentate on general personal development. And some executive education aims at developing the *breadth of perspective* and the *self-knowledge* required for successful leadership.

All of these courses make executives more valuable to their companies. Not incidentally, all of them make executives more likely to succeed in their personal career goals and less likely to find themselves swept aside by time and change.

THE EXECUTIVE LEADERSHIP SERIES

The institute's first major effort was the Executive Leadership Series, which includes a series of programs lasting from three days to one week.

Programs One and Two have already been given to the top 300 executives in BellSouth. The two programs combined into a one-week program have been given to the top 1200 managers and executives. Program Three is now being given to those at the top of the firm and will eventually be given to other executives and managers.

Program One: The Leadership Challenge

Program One is called The Leadership Challenge. No more than twenty participants are involved at any one time, and *involved* is certainly the word for the experience. In an intense forty-seven-hour week, the executives read Plato, live in the wilderness, and grapple with the meaning of leadership as both an abstract principle and concrete, personal behavior. Because of its intensity and because executives spend three days in the wilderness, Program One is fondly referred to at BellSouth as the "Rambo" program. Its objectives are:

- To develop a strong sense of what leadership is and its importance to BellSouth.
- To understand what is required to improve personal leadership competency.
- To understand the importance of ethics and values in leadership.

In explaining the use of the outdoors, Moore noted that "simulation programs are excellent, but only up to a point. Even the highly sophisticated simulation cannot anticipate the unexpected. Anything can and does happen in the outdoors. It provides a different type of learning and one that is more real, more spontaneous, and more vivid."

BellSouth's outdoor program requires participants to live and work outdoors for three days. They are given real-life tasks—such as leading a team to a destination in the allotted time—tasks that require teamwork and creativity. Moore believes the outdoor session provides an excellent learning environment because it is realistic. For instance, people must deal with time constraints and inadequate resources, just as they do at work. Yet the outdoors also has the advantage of confronting participants with tasks unfamiliar to them. They can't get by on technical know-how or subject-matter expertise, as they often do on the job. To complete the tasks successfully, they can rely on nothing but their leadership skills and teamwork. Furthermore, the consequences of their leadership—good or bad—are immediate. People know instantly whether or not they were successful and can then analyze what went well, what could have been done better. Teams are debriefed after each exercise; their positive behaviors are reinforced and their negative behaviors pointed out so individuals can learn to correct them. The next step is capturing the implications for improving their effectiveness as leaders back home.

The second part of Program One puts the same group of executives in a seminar-type setting. With the assistance of a moderator who guides them through an open-ended, Socratic questioning process, participants are encouraged to enter a candid discussion of their reactions to a group of readings related to leadership. Some of the readings are philosophical, some political, some economic, some scientific, and some religious. Writers discussed have included Plato, Dostoyevski, Aldous Huxley, Lincoln, Thoreau, Milton Friedman, and Martin Luther King, Jr.

The seminar discussions offer the opportunity to look at the role that values play in leadership. They encourage examination of the moral and ethical dilemmas faced by leaders throughout time and of the challenge, nature, and responsibilities of positive and forceful leadership. The discussions also acknowledge the ethical and value-related challenges to corporate culture.

The difficulty in measuring the success of this part of the program is that participants find it hard to articulate exactly how they have been affected. "[A]lthough they can't always tell us how they have been affected," said Moore, "we see and hear reports of how an individual has changed for the better by becoming a better listener, or being more tolerant of subordinates, or involving subordinates and colleagues in the decisionmaking process."

By taking part in the humanities portion of Program One, individuals gain an appreciation for personal integrity and values as applied to business issues. By gaining personal perspective, participants are better able to see the moral and ethical issues involved in their business decisions, and they realize the relevance and need to incorporate their personal values into decisions that involve compromise. "No one can be so rigid that they have a long list of values from which they never deviate in making a decision, but there need to be some core values from which they will not deviate," said Moore. "The executive must understand how decisionmaking can be influenced by the conflict between principles and expediency."

Executives must also weigh their own personal and professional values against those held by others in the company. A successful executive realizes how influential personal values are—not only on himself but on others—and strengthens his or her own leadership skills by better understanding others' points of view.

On the final day of Program One, participants review the specific behaviors and attitudes that distinguish an excellent BellSouth executive from his or her peers.

Program Two: Personal Excellence

In Program Two, which lasts two-and-a-half days, executives study and examine their own personal awareness of what a leader is and how they can best develop a personal leadership style that compliments and supports the core values of BellSouth. The program is called Personal Excellence: Living Our Values; as the title implies, its aim is to help executives "walk like they talk." Its objectives are to help participants:

- Understand the meaning and intent of BellSouth's core values.
- Know the attitudes and behaviors that distinguish excellent leaders from their peers and that are important to achieving personal excellence.
- Know how they are perceived by subordinates and peers in terms of demonstrating the attitudes and behaviors associated with excellence at BellSouth.
- Better understand different leadership styles and the way to select the best style for a particular situation.
- Understand how to use practical tools that can help them better achieve excellence in day-to-day leadership.
- Come up with innovative ideas for achieving excellence in the entire corporation.
- Develop an action plan for desired changes in behavior back on the job.

It is the aim of Program Two to take general corporate values and show how they can be translated into practical, specific guidelines for daily behaviors, thereby creating a bridge between existing managerial competencies and evolving corporate needs, as reflected in the BellSouth's values and their interpretation.

Prior to attending the program, managers are sent copies of the BellSouth Leadership Inventory. This questionnaire, which is to be completed to the manager's peers and subordinates, allows those who work with and for the manager to express opinions about his or her effectiveness in carrying out the BellSouth values and key leadership practices. Through the inventory, participants receive feedback on how they are perceived by peers and/or subordinates. The questionnaires are anonymous and are sent to an outside consultant for analysis.

In a one-on-one session, each participant is told candidly and confidentially how he or she has been assessed; each then develops a personal action plan for improvement. No one other than the participant and the outside consultant handling the analysis has access to this information. The process is solely for the benefit of the participant.

In the rest of the program, participants learn how to determine and use the appropriate leadership style for each of their subordinates. They learn and practice the skills needed to enhance leadership effectiveness. The program is so effective that it receives nearly perfect scores on participant evaluations.

Program Three: Achieving Peak Performance

Program Three, which at the time of writing was being developed for the top 300 BellSouth executives, is entitled Achieving Peak Performance. Its objective is to help participants achieve peak performance personally and from their subordinates by:

- Developing skills that help achieve personal peak performance.
- Enhancing day-to-day leadership.
- Learning a practical performance management process to help employees achieve peak performance.
- Learning how to coach employees for increased performance, learning, and enjoyment.
- Developing action plans to improve personal and staff performance back on the job.

Subjects covered include providing performance feedback in a timely manner; coaching, making people "feel like winners," giving performance feedback, encouraging employee development, motivating others, dealing with diverse people and styles of working, and confronting and dealing with conflicts among people.

In addition, participants again receive feedback on the BellSouth Leadership Inventory to see what progress they have made since Program Two.

THE BENEFITS OF ONGOING EDUCATION

There is no question about it. The BellSouth Management Institute has been an extraordinary success. The new BellSouth began operating on January 1, 1984. By 1986, the BellSouth Management Institute was up, running, and contributing to the company's successful entry into the world of fierce competition. By 1988, it had become institutionalized. The most rewarding feedback has come from those skeptics who initially doubted the value of the institute but who, as participants, came to be believers:

I had to think more in those few days than I have had to in several years. Some of my values are stronger by having them challenged; others I am not sure about. I intend to do more in the future on my own to be intellectually stimulated.

I was very skeptical about this program having practical application before it started. This skepticism was unfounded. It has given me the tools and the insight and the motivation to improve my leadership skills.

Before attending this program, I had severe doubts about its usefulness. This experience, despite my preconceived notions, turned out to be one of the most unique learning experiences I have encountered.

It [Management Institute] brought a totally different perspective to leadership. It made me think about what I really believe.

That type of feedback is music to Moore's ears. "Our ability to operate successfully in our future competitive environment is dependent upon how our people respond to it," he said. "Programs we have created in the Management Institute are a good way to help our executives deal with the changes that need to be made."

Moore is quick to point out that the most important reasons for the institute's success were John Clendenin's vision and commitment and the support of the entire senior management team. "There is no question that the program—and the company—is stronger because of the level of support we have received from top management," Moore said. "They have helped to create an environment in which the company attitude is that this program is successful, necessary, and helpful, so let's all get behind it and encourage it to become even stronger." That commitment from top management sets BellSouth's Management Institute apart from many other executive development plans, which Moore believes get only lip service from the upper corporate ranks.

Moore's advice to others given a similar opportunity?

First, make sure you have the commitment of senior management. If you don't, consider scaling back. You can only go as far as the CEO wants to go. Second, do a thorough needs analysis, and then develop a long-term strategy based on real need. In other words, identify the problem and *then* come up with the solution. And third, dare to dream, to be creative, to go beyond the traditional.

V A MAJOR CORPORATE TRANSFORMATION

9 THE WEYERHAEUSER FOREST PRODUCTS COMPANY

Charles ("Charley") Bingham might well be called the Lee Iacocca of the forest products industry. As the chief executive officer of the Weyerhaeuser Forest Products Company (FPC), Bingham and his executive team transformed a struggling organization into an effective competitor in a cyclical industry still plagued with oversupply. And like Iacocca, Bingham did it through tenacity—and plenty of candor.

Probably Bingham's most important—and toughest—assignment during the transformation was to "sell" the vision of what the company could be to the employees. For FPC to survive, its executive group had to convince the troops that a dramatic turnaround was possible.

To say that the employees were discouraged and pessimistic would be an understatement. "The attitude of our people was pretty close to being a total blue funk," says Bingham, in his typical candid style, describing morale in the company in 1985. "We had been through some very tough times throughout the industry. The entire attitude needed bombardment."

For that "bombardment," Bingham and his top executives turned to executive development. "We had a sense that we needed to do something that would give us purpose, esprit, teamwork, and rekindle a spark in the organization," explains Bingham. Executive development—which eventually took form as the Leadership Institute—was to provide the unifying vision, the enhanced knowledge base, the new skills, leadership, and teamwork that were necessary to bring FPC from where it was barely surviving—to where it could be—profitable and positioned for growth in the global marketplace.

CHANGES IN THE FOREST PRODUCTS INDUSTRY

The employees had good reason to be skeptical about the possibility of a recovery. Like the American automobile industry, the American forest products industry was undergoing wrenching change. The worst recession since the Great Depression had taken its toll in the early 1980s. Unlike previous downturns, that one came with very high interest rates, which put construction projects on hold. High inflation aggravated the situation. There was also a severe oversupply of forest products. But that nightmare was, as it turned out, only the tip of the iceberg.

A cyclical industry, forest products was accustomed to the ups and downs of the marketplace. Despite the severity of the downturn, that factor in itself was not what put FPC into "a total blue funk." What was also undoing employees' confidence in the company and in themselves was a longer term, irreversible phenomenon: the changing face of competition, both domestic and global. For those changes, FPC was unprepared.

Until the early 1980s, FPC's main competition was only other large, integrated American companies, such as Georgia-Pacific, Boise Cascade, and Champion International. Like FPC, they had been weakened by the recession. Some large companies, particularly in the western United States, were beginning to deemphasize forest products and were selling that part of their businesses to small owners, or in some cases to employee cooperatives.

Therefore, within a short period, a new form of competition reared its head: small, entrepreneurial, nonunionized, owner-operated companies. Because of their size, they could be highly responsive to the marketplace. Their cost structure was low. They were able to buy equipment at fire-sale rates from those companies going out of business. As a result, they could be fiercely competitive in pricing. That positioned them to wage "guerrilla warfare" on their larger, more traditional competitors. And they were prepared for a long siege.

The new competitors' profit margins tended to be high because, unlike some of the integrated giants in the industry, many of them offered specialized products; that is, instead of just selling the customer a tree, they focused on specific products to meet customer needs in particular market niches. That value-added dimension made products more marketable and profitable, despite the overcapacity in the industry. And as owner-operated businesses, their staff motivation and morale were high.

Internationally, FPC's competitive positioning was being eroded by the sustained strength of the dollar. Exports became more expensive at the same time that imports into the United States were priced lower than ever. That was happening at a time when export was a very important part of its business.

THE TRANSFORMATION OF FPC

To cope with the downturn and the new comeptitive forces, the Weyerhaeuser Company, FPC's corporate parent, made significant structural and strategic changes. Those changes included a massive reorganization. Weyerhaeuser had gone from being a highly centralized organization to a decentralized one. Decisionmaking was pushed down to three new operating companies, of which the Weyerhaeuser Forest Products Company was one. Essentially, the parent became like a holding company, and the operating companies were to be highly autonomous.

FPC was simultaneously downsized, reducing many layers of management. That dramatically cut overhead and those managerial employees who were retained faced salary freezes. The wages and benefits of some unionized employees also had to be rolled back. In addition, the strategic direction was shifted. Like some of the entrepreneurial competitors, FPC planned to go from being a producer of raw materials or commodities to a marketer of specialized products. Bingham explains that the key to doing this is to "*differentiate* our products, either produced or sold, in such a way that we add an *extraordinary value* [for] the customers we are serving."

"The dimension of this change is *huge*," says Bingham.

Approximately 80 percent of our sales dollars in 1982 represented products sold as commodities. By 1995 we have resolved that we must *reverse* the proportions so that 80 percent of our sales dollars will be in products sold by us as differentiated products, and only about 20 percent of our sales dollars will be in products sold as commodities.

The restructuring was a step in the right direction—but only a step. Moreover, the ability of the organization to implement its new strategic direction was being undercut by the pervasive poor morale. Many middle managers were pessimistic about the possibility of sustained future success.

Theoretically, the decentralization positioned FPC to be more responsive to the marketplace and to generate better profit margins from specialties versus commodities. The new organization consisted of about 200 profit centers, with each center being largely responsible for its own bottom line.

Before that improved positioning could yield results, however, Bingham and his team realized that there would have to be a total transformation of the organization—its corporate culture, knowledge base, skills level, style of leadership, and team orientation. "We had to change the whole way we thought about the business—from being . . . primarily a raw-material manufacturing organization, which characterized us in all our eighty years of history, to being primarily a customer- and market-driven organization."

For example, since the new organization was a collection of stand-alone profit centers, the executives and managers would have to learn how to run their units at a profit. But at the time, few of them had any experience in being responsible for a total business, or for the profit-and-loss statement.

In addition, the company had a long tradition of being resource-driven. Its executives would have to shift from that inward focus to one that reached outward to the customer and the marketplace. In short, FPC would have to make the leap from being a "tree-growing" company to an entrepreneurial organization that could market value-added products. But few executives understood the complexities of "value"—what it was, how to create it, what pricing policies should apply to it, and how to use it to gain and keep the competitive advantage.

"We felt that we needed some management skills that we just simply hadn't developed very well over a twenty-year period," observes Bingham. "Secondly, we needed some real help on how you approach managing a company from the marketplace backwards."

But experience suggested the need to avoid rushing into a quick fix. His goal was not to "convert" a handful of top executives to the new vision of being a market-driven rather than a production-driven company. "What we needed," Bingham stresses, "was for the *whole* organization to 'buy into' the new strategic direction."

To meet this need, the executive team took a risk. They decided to use a formal executive development program as a tool to transform and revitalize a complex organization. In 1986, the FPC Executive Team launched the Leadership Institute.

CREATING THE LEADERSHIP INSTITUTE

To do the job right—to get a high-quality program—FPC would have to invest a substantial amount of money and time. And the top management group would have to convince all the company's executives that this was not simply throwing resources, including money, at a difficult problem and hoping to pull off a miracle.

How the organization was sold on the worth of an executive development program is an important lesson. The trump card used in closing the deal was to involve the executives at various levels of organization in the planning stages. During those stages, they came to see, as did the executive team that an intensive development program such as the Leadership Institute was not an expensive frill but a prerequisite for survival. The Leadership Institute, top management was convinced, would be a powerful catalyst that could accelerate the normal process of change—of everything from a corporate culture to how a salesperson deals with customers.

Bingham established three criteria for the institute. He told Horace Parker, who was given the assignment of heading up the institute: "One, we need quality. Two, something that is innovative in the learning process to 'grab' the participants' attention—to jolt them out of their familiar ways of thinking about the business. And, three, all the learning has to be applicable and directly transferable to the job."

One important goal of the Leadership Institute, Bingham continually stressed, was changing attitudes. On a number of occasions, Bingham told Parker, "It [is] critically important to change the attitude from 'Oh, I got all these problems and how can I ever see my way out of the bottom of the barrel,' to one of a strong sense of personal conviction that we [can] manage our own destiny."

Phase One: Research and Analysis

The human resource staff then launched phase one—the research and analysis phase—of the Leadership Institute. (For a schematic description of the Leadership Institute's development process, see Figure 9–1.)

Figure 9–1.   Weyerhaeuser Leadership Institute
Development Process.

PHASE	PROCESS	OUTPUT
Research & Analysis	• Research, study, and analyze available information about the organization • Conduct a needs analysis by interviewing a sample of potential participants and "experts"	• A report of findings and recommendations including: – Program objectives, subject matter, and parameters – Objectives for each subject – Other management issues
Program Design	• Develop creative approaches/ alternatives for "delivering" the program objectives and subject matter	• A report including recommended: – Sequencing of subjects – Daily schedule – Descriptions of each program unit (subject) including specific topics to be covered under each subject • Preliminary thoughts on teaching methods and faculty
Material Development and Faculty Sourcing	• Select and/or develop learning materials • Test materials as needed • Locate, screen, schedule, and prepare faculty	• Participant materials • Teaching materials • Teaching plans • Faculty selected
Pilot Program	• Test program by conducting it with actual participants • Facilitate program • Revise topics, materials, and faculty based on the pilot results	• Required design revisions • Revised participant/teaching materials • Faculty changes as required

Note: Formal reviews are to be conducted with the Steering Committee at the end of each phase to approve and finalize results.

This phase consisted of surveying a cross-section of executives at FPC to find out, in detail, what they thought was needed to implement the new strategic direction. Bingham asked several executives to form a steering committee, which represented a broad cross-section of top management. Working with an outside consultant and Parker, the steering committee was in an ideal position to determine where the organization was in terms of attitudes, knowledge base, and skills.

After the research and analysis was completed, the members of the steering committee would help analyze what gaps existed between where the organization was and where the organization should be. They also had responsibility for making sure that the program would be tailored to FPC's immediate needs, that is, that it would be no "ivory tower" approach to learning. Equally important, they were to be the watchdogs: monitoring progress and seeing to it that the program stayed on track.

The formation of the steering committee while the institute was in the very early planning stages created a sense of ownership among those key executives. Since they were helping to shape the institute, they became its sponsors. And their sponsorship gave the program immediate credibility among all managers.

Bingham fully realized how crucial their support would be. He stressed that unless senior executives—including himself—were committed to the institute, the program would never get off the ground because, "First of all, you can't measure immediately its added value, you simply can't. Secondly, you have a lot of front-end cost if you want to do it right. . . . Unless the senior executives, particularly the CEO, say, 'This is important and we're going to do it,' it just won't happen."

Bingham had made it clear that he didn't want a smorgasbord-type program. He stressed the importance of developing a number of top priorities and then doing those well. FPC's experience in management development during the 1960s and 1970s showed him, Bingham admits, "how not to do it." The previous education programs tried teaching everything and anything. The curriculum had essentially reflected the instructors' pet theories and the then-popular management fads. Any overlap with the organization's needs was almost accidental.

Tons of data streamed in from the initial written survey of seventy executives followed by one-on-one interviews conducted by the consultants. Together, the steering committee, Parker, and the consultants analyzed the data and came up with a set of objectives for the institute:

- To build a market/customer-driven enterprise
- To build unity of purpose by communicating and strengthening commitment to FPC's vision, values, and principles
- To improve leadership skills and instill a sense of responsibility for leading FPC into the future
- To develop a broad business perspective and business ownership attitudes and competencies
- To become more creative and innovative in running the business

- To develop communication, cooperation, and a sense of teamwork across unit lines

The research and analysis phase served two crucial functions. First of all, it led to a statement of clearly defined objectives. That established the direction for the institute. Second, it gave all the participants—from the steering committee members to the survey respondents—a genuine feeling of ownership. Through their enthusiasm, they sold their colleagues on the value of attending the institute.

At the end of the research and analysis process, it was decided that the actual training would be divided into four one-week segments. The segments would be spaced four months apart. The four-month intervals between the four weeks of actual training were to provide time for executives to apply the new knowledge, skills, and behaviors to the real world of FPC and the marketplace.

Given the competitive threat, there was no time for the theoretical learning that more traditional executive development and most executive-MBA programs offer. Both Bingham and his top executives continually stressed that "all of the learnings be applicable and transferable to the job. . . . The effectiveness of the one-week training followed by four-month intervals is based on the fact that the institute doesn't go away. It's on people's minds, and they know that four months later they're going to come back. . . . Certain commitments, like that one . . . cause people to get things done."

It was decided that the top 200 persons in the organization would attend the institute. (That number was later increased to 600 because of the dramatic and rapid results that the program was having.) The participants in the institute would be divided into groups of twenty. Those twenty people would stay together as a group throughout the four weeks of the program. That would provide, explains Edward P. Rogel, vice-president of human resources, "a forum for networking and strengthening working relationships . . . an opportunity for those in different functions to learn from one another."

To help break down the barriers between functions, each group of twenty was structured to include a broad cross-section of executives from different functions. Although FPC had fewer layers of management after the reorganization, the boundaries between functions, as in many large organizations, were still impediments to the operating unity of the company. Because FPC had long been a production company, there was a history of conflict between those in manufacturing and those in marketing. For the new vision to become a reality, those cross-functional tensions had to give way to teamwork. Since that was not going to happen by osmosis or good intentions alone, the institute's curriculum included modules that helped participants see what real teamwork was and how to make it an operational, day-to-day reality.

Phase Two: Design

The second development stage was design. Four design committees were formed, and each was responsible for one week of the program. Each committee's members had to have technical expertise in the subjects covered during the week. For instance, those in marketing oversaw the structure of the curriculum for Week Two, which concentrated on market and customer issues. Again, the involvement of those with expertise generated among them a sense of ownership, in addition to ensuring the accuracy and relevance of the program material.

Among the design committees' decisions was how to approach and package the learning. Top management made it clear that they wanted to get and keep the participants' attention by using innovative approaches. The goal for the instruction methodologies used was to hurl executives far enough from their comfort zones that they would be forced to look for new ways of solving problems and identifying opportunities.

Phase Three: Material Development/ Faculty Sourcing

The third phase in the development process was developing and selecting materials and preparing the appropriate faculty. Most faculty came from either the nation's top graduate schools of business or leading consulting firms.

Phase Four: The Pilot Program

The fourth phase was the pilot program, which would be the acid test as to what worked and what didn't. There was a pilot session for each of the four weeks, and the steering committee members went through all of them.

Given the amount of planning that went into the Leadership Institute, it should be no surprise that, as Rogel reports, "we got 80 percent of it right the first time through." That other 20 percent was revised with help from the steering committee. The second group of "students" to attend the institute included Charley Bingham and his top team.

Figure 9–2. Weyerhaeuser Leadership Institute: Growing the FPC Team of Leaders.

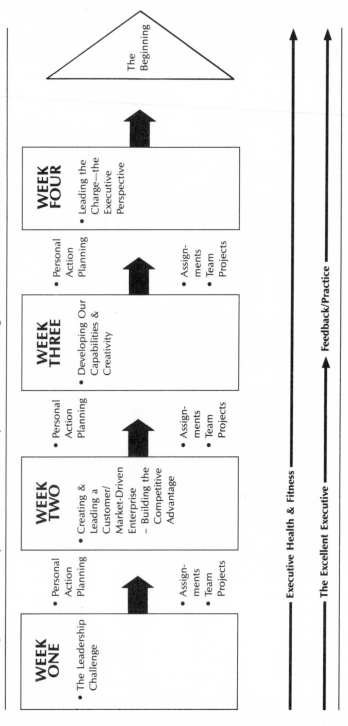

WEEK ONE
• The Leadership Challenge
• Personal Action Planning
• Assignments
• Team Projects

WEEK TWO
• Creating & Leading a Customer/Market-Driven Enterprise – Building the Competitive Advantage
• Personal Action Planning
• Assignments
• Team Projects

WEEK THREE
• Developing Our Capabilities & Creativity
• Personal Action Planning
• Assignments
• Team Projects

WEEK FOUR
• Leading the Charge—the Executive Perspective

The Beginning

Executive Health & Fitness

The Excellent Executive — Feedback/Practice

Each of the four weeks has a different theme. (See Figure 9–2.)

WEEK ONE: THE LEADERSHIP CHALLENGE

Since everyone agreed that strong leadership would be the foundation for the transformation of FPC, it was decided that leadership issues should be the focus of Week One. The objectives of the week are:

- To develop a strong sense of what leadership is and its importance and role in shaping and guiding FPC
- To understand what is required to improve personal leadership competency and to acquire the knowledge and commitment to do so
- To develop a strong sense of teamwork, unity of purpose, and esprit de corps
- To understand top management's vision of FPC's future

Week One's program is oriented toward jarring participants out of familiar ways of thinking—getting them to see leadership and teamwork in new ways—through experiential learning. The first two and a half days cover simulated outdoor challenges—such as rescuing an "injured" mountain climber. The exercises are structured so that no participant has any special expertise in the skills needed for success. That throws participants out of their personal and professional comfort zones and shocks them into being open to new learning, since they have little in their previous experience to fall back on. They are forced to deal with the present circumstances with new perspectives and skills. Otherwise they will fail.

As a result, principles of leadership and teamwork are laid bare. Rapid and thorough feedback is built into the exercises, often making comprehension of these principles immediate and gut-level. Executives literally shake their heads and say to themselves, or out loud, "Yeah, I get it."

The outdoor exercises used in the program differ from those associated with the Outward Bound program, which often focuses more on individual physical and mental challenges. In contrast, the outdoor experiences in the Leadership Institute focus on leadership and teamwork. The goal is to discover what leadership is, and what makes it effective or ineffective for a particular group. That, of course, takes into account the evolving corporate culture. Participants get a look at styles of leadership that seem to work and then ask themselves: Would that work at FPC? If not, why not?

A typical exercise during Week One centers on locating a "critically injured victim" on a mountain cliff and then removing him from the cliff within ninety minutes. A leader is selected for each team and is given a map that will help the team find its way to the site of the accident. Within minutes, team members are organizing themselves via constant, rapid instructions from walkie-talkies. As they ascend the mountain, dirt flies into their faces. They run into obstacles and figure out how to get around them. They strain to remain calm and focus as their deadline moves closer. To speed things up, they reorganize who's doing what.

In most cases, the team does make the rescue within the time allotted. Debriefing follows the exercise. There is extensive feedback, from both the participants and the faculty members. For example, one group commented that its leader's strong points included his ability to get lots of input from the team. His major weak point was allowing confusion to persist about the team members' particular roles.

In reflecting on their experiences during the outdoor exercises, participants frequently come to the realization that how leaders are perceived is as important as what they actually do or don't do. For instance, when one leader handed over the walkie-talkies to someone else, he was perceived as losing control. Another frequent comment is about the close relationship between values and style of leadership. That insight leads to discussion at the end of the week about what characteristics and essential values the "excellent executive" in the forest products industry should possess.

To build a bridge between the outdoor exercises and the discussions that follow in the next two days, a former prisoner-of-war comes to the institute and shares his experience in overcoming adversity. That brings to the surface other aspects of leadership, such as creativity, determination, and personal energy. People see that their problems and challenges pale by comparison.

Under the title, "Leaders of Humanity," the next two days are an exploration of personal and corporate values and their relationship to leadership. The participants, in Socratic fashion, use readings of classical and contemporary leaders as catalysts for discussion. They test their views against those of leaders and thinkers from Plato to Machiavelli to Martin Luther King. Participants struggle with the difficult subject of reconciling values with the pressure of circumstances and expediency. Is it okay to deviate from those values? Is expediency a valid justification for compromising an organization's traditional values? What are the clear signals that values need to be changed or updated? How can one avoid convenient rationalizations?

Men and women in leadership positions from a range of fields, including federal and state government, law, civil rights, the women's movement, business, and politics, come to this portion of the program and discuss their views. That diversity of viewpoints challenges the FPC executives. They are exposed to perspectives from well beyond their narrow, everyday corporate world. During this session participants learn not only the importance of a strong set of values but how they impact them as a leader.

In the next session, faculty and participants explore a model for the "excellent executive" at the new FPC. The model presents FPC's values translated into specific activities and behaviors; it also describes the leadership practices required for success in FPC's new corporate environment. During their time back on the job, and when they return to the institute for Week Three, participants will evaluate themselves against that model and will learn how they are perceived by others.

Before returning to the workplace, participants establish a personal action plan. They choose two or three behaviors that they want to modify during the next four months. They will monitor their progress with entries into workbooks handed out at the institute.

Teams of three to six participants also select a project to work on back on the job. Ideas for the projects come from sharing key insights gained from the week's program. The projects are aimed at business problems or opportunities that participants believe are significant and that require the application of the knowledge and skills they have developed during Week One. Those projects are expected to bring real results. In fact, the organization perceives them to be little different from any other important job assignment. After Weeks Two and Three, participants will again create personal action plans and select a team action project.

These projects have helped FPC executives solve hundreds of actual problems and identify and pursue as many opportunities. In addition to ensuring a direct transfer of learning from the institute, the personal action plans and team projects create a bridge between each of the four weeks of training.

There are also assignments between weeks. For example, between Week One and Week Two participants are responsible for being alert to their behaviors, both at work and away from work, that support or undermine the goals and values of a customer/market-driven organization. They also read material on marketing do's and don'ts. They write down their observations, to be used in Week Two.

The institute's holistic approach includes stressing the importance of health and physical fitness. Participants can elect to set up personal fitness goals ranging from certain kinds and amounts of exercise to acquiring better eating habits, to preventing the buildup of stress. They pursue their fitness goals throughout the twelve months of their participation in the institute. Although the Leadership Institute moves to a different geographical setting for each of the four weeks, the facilities always include a fitness staff. During Week One participants can have a comprehensive assessment of their physical fitness. In Weeks Two, Three, and Four there are sessions on topics like nutrition and stress. At the end of the institute, participants have an opportunity to check their progress toward their fitness goals.

WEEK TWO: CREATING AND LEADING A CUSTOMER/MARKET-DRIVEN ENTERPRISE

Week Two focuses on the competitive advantages of a customer/market-driven organization. There are four objectives for the week:

1. To understand the value of FPC's intention to become the customer/market-driven industry leader
2. To acquire a strong, realistic vision of what is required to become the industry leader
3. To understand in detail how to build and sustain a competitive advantage
4. To become committed to specific personal and organizational action that will advance and accelerate the company's effort

Week Two has a feature that is so unique—intensive feedback from actual customers—that it will be discussed at greater length in Chapter 10. The following is only a brief synopsis of FPC's innovative format for involving customers.

For four days, FPC executives and customers attend lectures together, participate in workshops, and even form teams together for the weeks' computer simulation. They eat together, work out in the fitness center together, share a few beers, and see each other again at 8:00 a.m. every morning. In short, there is no place for customers or FPC participants to "hide" from each other.

With the customers as learning partners, FPC executives explore the following issues:

- The need to become customer/market-driven
- How the industry and marketplace are changing and what should be expected in the future
- Determining what customers want and why
- How to forge profitable partnerships with customers by delivering a superior value at a profit
- Assessing FPC's corporate culture in relation to becoming a customer/market-driven enterprise

Week Two begins with reports by participants on their individual and team projects, followed by market analysis of other companies, both successful and unsuccessful ones. They review current FPC customer relations practices. Marketing experts present information and models that can be immediately applied to both FPC and the customers' businesses.

That information is used in workshops aimed at applying what has been learned to the working relationship with the customers. For example, one workshop focuses on identifying FPC's key customer/market segments and then determining the critical factors for success in those segments.

During the next phase of the workshop, participants look at the ability of FPC and its competitors to deliver on what is considered essential to success. The workshop ends with an assessment of FPC's key points of leverage in the marketplace, as well as its potential leverage. For example, customers frequently explain how FPC could beat out the competition by adding value not only to the product but through service.

Participants learn in detail what is critical to the customers' success. They learn how the customers' businesses operate and what the end-users need and expect. The goal of the discussions is to work out concrete plans for better serving the customers' and end-users' real needs. Follow-up plans, such as visiting customers' facilities, are made.

The last workshop is a computer simulation in which four quarters of an actual businesses's activity are compressed into a day. The simulation exercise is customized to reflect market conditions in the forest products industry. Four teams—each one made up of five FPC executives and one customer—compete with one another. The software is rigged so that to gain and keep the competitive advantage, teams have to apply the week's learnings.

Feedback is rapid. Within a half-hour of each quarter's end, every team receives computerized reports on how their businesses did versus their competitors (the other teams). That rapid feedback reinforces learning while the teams are still engrossed in what they have done in the simulation exercise—or, more importantly, not done. The insights they gain are applied at the end of the week to a critique of how FPC is positioned in the market.

Customers leave after the simulation, and the participants then discuss FPC's corporate culture in terms of being customer- and market-focused. Through facilitators, participants peel away layer after layer of assumptions—both positive and negative—about what kind of corporate culture prevails at FPC. They attempt to see the real strengths and weaknesses of its marketing methods. Then they identify the changes that need to be made if the company is to become a leader in the marketplace.

As with Week One, participants develop personal action plans and team projects to work on during the next four months.

WEEK THREE: DEVELOPING CAPABILITIES AND CREATIVITY

During Week Three participants apply the principles that they have learned in Weeks One and Two to an evaluation of the organization, their particular units, and themselves. The major objectives for the week are:

- To review progress on becoming customer/market-oriented and to determine what more needs to be done
- To understand how to be personally more creative and how to stimulate creativity on the job
- To understand the Weyerhaeuser "excellent executive" model and to receive feedback on personal strengths and areas for improvement
- To develop plans for improving personal capability and creativity

Horace Parker does a good job at summing up what Week Three is all about: "Essentially what we're doing in Week Three is looking at our vision of how to serve the customer, integrity, teamwork, and innovation. We put this all together and come up with an ideal of what kind of leaders FPC should have."

To help executives see themselves as others see them, participants get feedback from bosses, peers, and subordinates back on the job, using a leadership inventory. As Bingham tells participants, "The Weyerhaeuser Forest Products Company Leadership Inventory has been designed to reinforce the attitudes and behaviors that the company sees as most important."

Prior to Week Three, the participants select a range of FPC people to evaluate their effectiveness as a leader and manager. Those selected confidentially complete the leadership inventory, which is derived from the excellent executive model presented at the end of Week One. That model was an articulation of the behaviors that the "excellent executive" adheres to in carrying out corporate values. For instance, the "excellent executive" acts on the company's commitment to the customer by:

Serving the customer:
> Knows who his or her customers are
> Is dedicated to meeting the needs of people who use the company's services or products
> Encourages and listens to input from the people who use the company's services or products
> Acts to solve customers' problems in a timely manner

Building customer importance:
> Consistently treats the users of the company's products or services as a top priority
> Clearly communicates the importance of the people who use the company's products or services
> Does not allow destructive comments about the people who use the company's products or services
> Is more committed to the customers' long-term satisfaction than to the company's short-term gain

These behaviors appear on the leadership inventory as the aspects of performance on which the executive is evaluated. Subordinates and peers rate the executive on each behavior on a scale of one to five, from "highly dissatisfied" to "highly satisfied." A more open-ended write-in section is also provided.

Confidentiality is protected in two ways. First of all, the results are processed by computer outside the company. The participants receive only the computerized report. Secondly, the contents of the reports are shared by the faculty and facilitators only with the participant in one-on-one coaching sessions.

Throughout the rest of the week, there are modules on how participants can bring their attitudes, skills, and behavior closer to the ideal for effective leadership. Here are a few reactions from participants to the feedback part of Week Three:

> I realize now that I'm a role model. People will respond not to what I say but to what I do.

> People think I'm okay—effective as a leader—but what irks them is that I never admit when I'm wrong.

> I think now it really starts with me. We are the company as far as our people are concerned.

The second major element of Week Three, through lectures, discussion, and application exercises, deals with creativity and innovation. People learn how to be more creative themselves and to encourage and nurture innovation in their teams. As one participant noted, "I discovered that the ability to be creative isn't innate—it can be learned."

An integral part of Week Three is the spouse program. Wives and husbands of executives come for the entire week and go through a mini-version of the entire four-week program. Parker asserts, "What the program is not—and I repeat, *is not*—is a token invite-your-spouse-to-a-dinner kind of deal." He describes the three objectives for the innovative spouse program:

1. To offer spouses a developmental experience of their own: "For instance, the outdoor exercises can help anyone become more effective at leading and at being a productive team member, whether that team is a family or an office."
2. To help spouses better understand FPC.
3. To enable spouses to actually experience what their husbands and wives are asked and expected to do on their jobs. "In particular, we wanted them to be aware of what stresses are created by an organization undergoing rapid and constant change."

The institute staff asked eight spouses to help design the week. Results showed that they did a terrific job. The program received high ratings from spouses, and Bingham keeps receiving notes from spouses who have attended the institute, commenting that the realization of what their husbands and wives do at FPC has brought the two closer together.

As with the previous weeks, Week Three ends with making personal action plans and setting team projects to be completed during the next four months.

WEEK FOUR: THE EXECUTIVE PERSPECTIVE

In Week Four, Parker explains, "everything comes together—leadership skills, customer partnerships, market analysis, and innovation." And the final element that ties things together is financial management from an entrepreneurial perspective.

The four objectives for Week Four are:

1. To develop the skills and confidence in participants to run their units as if the units were their own businesses, that is, to encourage all executives to take an entrepreneurial approach. [Like their small competitors in the forest products industry, executives learn to run their units like owner-operated businesses.]
2. To understand how to run a total business—rather than just a component of a business—in a manner that contributes to both customer and FPC profitability. [The goal of running the business should be enhancing the profit partnership between FPC and the customer.]
3. To develop a strong sense of teamwork in confronting the common challenges and opportunities. [This objective underscores the need to break down functional barriers.]
4. To assimilate the lessons learned from the Leadership Institute in a way that optimizes commitment to the company and its direction, focuses action on the right issues, and inspires confidence. [Participants were ideally qualified to become change agents throughout the organization, communicating in detail the new strategic direction to all employees.]

Although many executives have some knowledge of financial concepts, they usually lack the skills to operate an actual business. Since authority and responsibility have been, as Bingham describes it, "pushed way, way out and down the organization," FPC executives and managers could no longer coast along on their other talents without coming to terms with business realities, such as profit-and-loss statements.

Faculty from a major university present the essentials of strategic financial management. They speak to the participants as if they were all sole owners of businesses. That model helps participants avoid assigning blame to their corporate parent for missed opportunities, declining profits, or an actual loss.

Simultaneously, participants shift to a can-do mindset. In launching the institute, Bingham and his top executives stressed that they wanted to replace the executives' negative outlook with a belief in their ability to shape their own destiny. Week Four is the final step in that transition from defeatism to a sense of control over the company's future.

After they have acquired the financial essentials, participants move on to a competitive business simulation. This time, though, financial variables are added. Several years of operations are condensed into two days. As with the earlier simulation, the software includes all the opportunities and constraints existing in the forest products industry. Teams compete for customers' sales and profits.

ENVISIONING THE FUTURE

Not long before the graduation ceremony, the participants engage in a visioning exercise. They are told that they have been invited to give a talk at the Harvard Business School. It's three years from today, and the subject is "How the Weyerhaeuser Forest Products Company Became an Incredible Success."

The participants work on the talk individually at first; then they share their thoughts in small teams. The teams work together preparing a skit, which provides an opportunity for different functions to compare visions of what their contribution could be in the long term. Equally important, participants can play with "what-if" scenarios and success fantasies about themselves and the company. The exercise helps participants envision what things will be like at FPC when they successfully apply what's been learned in the institute. Presentation of the skits to top management provides an exciting vision of FPC's future.

Those fantasies are already coming true. In 1987 the Weyerhaeuser Forest Products Company reported near-record sales of $3.2 billion, versus $2.6 billion for 1986. Pretax earnings for 1987 were $339 million, compared with $244 million for the previous year. Operating margins improved from 9.3 percent in 1986 to 10.4 percent in 1987. Its annual report for 1987 states, "The improved competitiveness enabled our operations to operate without any market interruption—for the first time since 1983."

Bingham admits that the ongoing success "can't all be attributed to executive development." For example, the weakening of the dollar has helped boost exports. He's convinced, however, that the institute has been a "powerful" catalyst for transforming the company:

There's more teamwork, *much, much* more teamwork. We can trace it specifically to experiences people have had in the institute. We can trace it specifically to the relationships which developed. You can trace it to the commitment the organization has made to teamwork.

Secondly, the whole attitude of "The world is falling in, how do we ever get out of this blue funk," has changed to one in which—and I don't want to be trite about this—90 percent of our folks are taking any particular problem and saying, "There must be an opportunity here somewhere."

Moving away from "soft areas," such as teamwork, Bingham reflects on bottom-line effects: "We have a couple of managers who have very large line-operating accountabilities who have made phenomenal bottom-line improvements within six months of attending Week One."

A follow-up study of over 200 persons who had attended the institute was conducted during June 1988. When asked about the personal results of participating in the institute, the respondents most frequently mentioned:

- Stronger leadership skills
- An increase in teamwork and group participation
- Improved working relationships with subordinates, including better communication, particularly in giving and receiving feedback
- A shift to a delegating/leading style of management; improved skills in coaching, providing autonomy, and giving positive reinforcement
- More focus on customer service, satisfaction, and relations

In terms of impact on effectiveness and performance, the respondents most frequently mentioned:

- An improvement in customer orientation; improved service and value for the customer
- Improved operations, effectiveness, and efficiency of employees
- Better budgeting of time and resources

The impact of the Leadership Institute continues to grow as more and more FPC executives attend it. By 1989, 600 executives will have completed four weeks of development. In addition, division-level versions of the program are being designed to spread this type of learning more widely throughout the organization.

Through top managements' confidence in the vision, the Leadership Institute was born. They were taking a risk. By using such an unconventional tool to transform a traditional corporate culture to an entrepreneurial one, they were putting their credibility—and their time and budget—on the line.

But the risk paid off—in ways that even Bingham didn't anticipate. "Some participants claim that it has changed their whole life," he says with amazement. "We had no idea that it would be this powerful."

10 BECOMING A CUSTOMER/ MARKET-DRIVEN ENTERPRISE

The rhetoric—or more accurately, the battle cry—of much of American business is to "keep close to the customer." That now common phrase was introduced by Thomas J. Peters and Robert H. Waterman, Jr. in *In Search of Excellence* back in the early 1980s. But the reality generally has been very different from the rhetoric.

What most American businesses seem to do, by default or by intention, is keep their customers at a safe distance. The so-called "getting input" from customers frequently takes place via surveys or focus groups—that is, in highly controlled contexts in which customers rarely have access to a cross-section of the corporation's executives and managers.

A few brave corporations have invited several customers for a half day at headquarters. But those visits—like visits from the media—are also carefully engineered. Other brave corporations have sent a few executives off to customers' places of business; but here again, the context is far from the heart of the corporation.

AN URGENT MISSION

For that reason, what Charley Bingham, and his top management team did in 1986 was unique—and potentially very risky. They invited *groups* of customers, both domestic and international, to meet with a cross-section of FPC's executives for the unheard-of time of *four days* during Week Two of the Leadership Institute.

How they have structured those visits—and there have already been about twenty of them—is equally unique. Since 1986, the customers have been attending Weyerhaeuser's executive development program side by side with the company's top 600 executives. Customers and executives go to lectures together, participate in workshops together, and form teams to compete in computer simulations.

FPC's goal in obtaining intense input from customers was also unusual. They did not want feedback merely so that FPC could fine-tune its relationship with customers. Their goal was much more ambitious. Bingham wanted to build ongoing "profit partnerships" between FPC and its customers. As partners working together, they could accomplish more than either could accomplish by working alone.

To achieve mutual success for both parties in the partnership, FPC and the customers would have to learn a great deal about each other's businesses, where the opportunities were, and how to overcome barriers to those opportunities.

A further difference between Bingham's strategy and what was standard back in 1986 was that his strategy for becoming a customer/market-driven organization was designed to affect everyone in the company, not just those with direct customer contact. "Understanding customer needs is everyone's business, not just the marketing people." Bingham feels as strongly about this as ever. "Our only reason to exist as a company is to serve customer needs and that requires everyone in the company on the oars together to do that." Given that broad definition of customer relations, it is no surprise that the executive development effort included executives from all functions, ranging from manufacturing to accounting.

The FPC top management team took this unconventional—and potentially risky—approach to getting "close to the customer" because their mission was aggressive and urgent. They were determined to transform FPC from a resource-oriented business to one that would be driven by the customer and the marketplace. That transformation was critical if FPC was to survive and thrive in the late 1980s and beyond.

CUSTOMER INVOLVEMENT: WOULD IT WORK?

When designing Week Two of the Leadership Institute, Bingham, the steering committee, and the outside consultants who were helping to shape the program were all, at first, as wary as most corporations would be about the scope of customer participation.

That wariness came from three concerns. The first concern was whether senior-level customers would be willing to take the time from their own business activities to meet with those at FPC.

The second concern was over the unpredictability of the situation, particularly since there were not many precedents for customer participation in a corporation's executive development program. What many corporate executives feared in soliciting customer input in a public forum was simply the possibility of being embarrassed by negative comments about their company.

In addition to the public embarrassment of negative feedback, a related concern was the impact on executives of personal criticism. They could become defensive, discouraged, and demoralized. What if one function attacked another as the cause of the problems—in front of the customers?

Furthermore, what if dissatisfaction among a group of customers gathered together became contagious? One customer's complaints might remind other customers of similar ones. As a result, they could all decide to go to the competition.

The third concern was a realistic fear that caution would rule—as it often did when customers came for other kinds of short visits. Nothing much would be said since customers did not want to undermine their relationships with their suppliers. Also, it is human not to want to "step on any toes"—particularly if those representing the functions under attack are present.

The first and third concerns evaporated quickly. When FPC felt out customers about coming, they were enthusiastic and, as it turned out, flattered to have been invited. In fact, they agreed to send their senior executives. A more important motivation to come, however, was their belief that the visit would give them a unique opportunity to influence one of their key suppliers.

The concern about not getting adequate or candid input would be alleviated by the structure of Week Two. The customers were invited to attend as full learning partners, the very concept of which encourages frank discussion.

Moreover, built into the week's activities were lectures and exercises that would generate in-depth analysis of what customers needed from FPC. For example, a module in which faculty work with participants to develop a model for the "ideal" market-driven company in the forest products industry is followed by workshops in which small groups made up of five FPC executives and a customer look at what changes FPC needs to make to fit that model, as perceived by the customer.

This format of lecture discussion followed by small-group workshops applying the concepts to the FPC-customer business relationship ensured the immediate testing and application to the marketplace of what was being learned.

Leaving the second concern—about the impact of the customer feedback—up in the air was a risk that Bingham and the steering committee were willing to take. But it still had to be decided how much risk FPC was willing to assume. Practically speaking, how long a visit should the customers have?

The first suggestion was one day. Two days soon seemed like a better idea, but then three days was successfully argued to be the best idea of all. Three was the final decision. The customers would leave before the fourth day's computer simulation of a forest industry competitive situation.

But that decision was changed—by the customers. Once they were exposed to the sessions, they saw that it was useful for their own learning—and for FPC executives' understanding of their business problems—if they took part in the simulation. They were therefore invited to stay for four days.

WEEK TWO: CREATING A CUSTOMER/ MARKET-DRIVEN ENTERPRISE

Horace Parker, describes Week Two's major objectives:

First of all, we needed to develop a commitment to building a competitive advantage as a key value of our company.

Secondly, we needed to build skills for understanding the marketplace, competition, and enhancing our unit strategies.

Third, we really needed to give our executives a boost in our transition from being resource-driven to market-driven.

Fourth, we needed a *very detailed* understanding of what it means to be customer-oriented. And how could we start putting in place plans to make that shift?

And, fifth, we needed guidance on what we had to do in terms of corporate culture to support that kind of shift. What are the cultural ramifications of making a shift from a resource orientation to a customer focus?

To achieve those objectives, six interrelated modules were designed for the week. Each module builds on the knowledge, insights, and skills acquired in previous modules. All faculty members for Week Two of the Leadership Institute are from either top-ranked university business schools or leading consulting firms.

Module One: New Corporate Values

Module One examines the corporate values that prevail at successful midsize companies. Faculty use lectures, case studies, and their own research to illustrate ten beliefs and behaviors that characterize current successful organizations. Those characteristics, they show, often clash with conventional formulas for success. In fact, those companies may be setting new traditions for how to be successful.

The faculty note that "new tradition" companies can be characterized by the following:

- They create and develop niches instead of only penetrating the biggest markets.
- Strategies based on value win out over strategies based exclusively on low pricing. As opposed to a narrow concept of *value* as a physical change in the commodity, new tradition companies have a broad concept of *value* that includes intangibles such as a company's brand names or service. Therefore, "value-added" could be the customers' perception of what benefit the product brought to their business.
- They edge out into related products and markets, instead of simply "minding their own business."
- They don't take a product they don't know to markets they don't know; they don't build conglomerates.
- Instead of telling employees what they need to do because employees always need to be told, they give employees values and a mission and make them shareholders.
- Their mission is to build a stronger institution, not solely to create wealth. This shifts attention from short-term financial results to longer term objectives.
- They believe you should fix it or it will break, not, "If it ain't broke, don't fix it."
- Rather than adopt a cool, detached professionalism, they are concerned with faith, instinct, intuition, facts, and analysis. In short, they reaffirm entrepreneurial values.

- With clear values and priorities and a strong culture, they do not focus exclusively on measurement systems, that is, profits. If executives take care of the *whole* company, everything—including profitability—will turn out right.

Those ten characteristics serve, during the rest of the week, as guidelines for analyzing how both FPC and its customers could better run their businesses—and how they could be better partners. The theme of "value" would prove to be particularly important. Throughout the four days, customers explore what value-addeds are important to them and to their customers, the end-users.

Module Two: Gaining Competitive Advantage

Module Two focuses on gaining competitive advantage. It is shown that meeting the customers' needs is not enough; meeting needs has to be done better, or in ways different from those of the competition. Customers give concrete suggestions on what FPC could be doing better or differently, and workshop exercises bring out highly detailed feedback.

Through those workshops, FPC executives then take a hard look at what customers want and need and how FPC is meeting or is not meeting those demands and needs. The primary focus is on what changes would have to be made at FPC to satisfy the customer better than the competition does. The FPC executives learn that it is also important to anticipate what value-addeds newly emergent competitors might offer.

Many of the recommendations for change mirror the ten characteristics of new tradition companies presented in the previous module. For instance, many participants concluded that FPC would have to take a longer term approach to managing the business and to building relationships with customers. They viewed the preoccupation with short-term financial performance as getting in the way of strategic planning and learning about customers and end-users. As one FPC executive commented,

Our corporate creed and culture started with the trees, not with the customer. If we take care of the customer and understand his needs and our costs, profits will follow, and we don't need to worry so much about the short-term. If you're going after a market—and you should be going after that market because you have the capability—the profits will follow in the long term. As we learned here, we have to keep our eye on the ball and not on the inning-by-inning score.

Module Three: Adding Value

In Module Three the focus is value: How is it created, and what does it contribute to the business success of both FPC and its customers? Two techniques for creating value are explored in depth—consultative selling and value-based pricing.

Through consultative selling, FPC was to shift from its focus on itself, the seller, to a focus on the needs of the buyer, its customers. In fact, a crucial insight gained in this module is that FPC's focus should not be exclusively just on its immediate customers but more often on the products' end-users, that is, FPC's customers' customers. That realization alone revolutionized the modus operandi throughout much of FPC and in many units of the customers' businesses.

In highly emotional statements, customers explained how FPC could be helping them—but wasn't:

> It's helpful to have backup from Weyerhaeuser in conveying a quality image to *our* customer. Sometimes the story is not as well taken from us as it would be from the actual manufacturer.

> This takes time but I still think that it's a good idea if we visit your mills and find out how products are produced so that we can understand what "value" you're adding. How can we sell our customers on the product's attributes unless we know what happens to the raw materials in the conversion process?

The second crucial piece of learning in Module Three is how to establish pricing policies based on value—that is, on the total benefits that products offer to customers. For example, as one FPC participant commented, "I see now that a customer will buy a two-by-four because of what *both* the two-by-four and the seller can do for him. And what we do for him has to be in some way superior or different from what the competition is doing."

That approach to pricing differs from conventional orientations, which focus on costs and what the competition is charging.

In mulling over what they were learning, one of the FPC executives observed during this workshop:

> "Value differentiation" forces me to think about the customer—that is, the needs of the buyer. The way I used to think—the product mentality—forces me to only consider the two-by-four. I see now that unless you have the right frame of reference and the right terminology, you're not going to ask the right questions. And it's crystal clear to me that if I think in terms of "value differentiation," I'm going to ask the right questions.

From the workshops, FPC executives come up with concrete strategies for how they would apply the model of value-based pricing to their products. In addition, they look at their corporate culture and formulate a list of barriers that would undermine the "value" approach to marketing. Finally, they make a set of recommendations to eliminate or lessen those impediments.

Because the executives have the organizational authority to implement those recommendations, the workshops are not mere brainstorming sessions. That is a key advantage of having top executives with the authority to make changes attend the institute.

Module Four: Applying the Lessons Learned

In Module Four, FPC executives and customers apply what they have just learned in a computer simulation of an actual business operating in the real world, which includes fierce competition in the marketplace. The program for that simulation incorporates the marketplace principles that have been discussed. The simulation is rigged to recognize and reward an adept application of those principles. Each team consists of both FPC executives and customers.

The teams organize themselves into "companies" that compete with one another for four quarters. They are given extensive background information, and after each simulated quarter they are given computerized results of how they are doing versus the other teams.

Typical of the decisions the teams have to make are: which markets to target; when to increase or reduce the sales force; where and by how much; how much money to spend on market research; how much to spend on advertising; and how much inventory to carry. The four-quarter format helps bring home to the participants the long-term impacts of present decisions.

FPC participants have offered the following observations on the computer simulation:

I saw the importance of prioritizing customers and how I should go about determining those priorities. Also, I saw the need to understand your competitors.

We won out by keeping our eye on the ball versus the per-quarter score. That meant that when we had short-term pricing opportunities, we didn't resort to gouging customers and alienating them. Another important thing that we did was look where we could create value—for example, through research and development—and in the long term get rewarded for it. We weren't the low-cost producer or supplier, but we did just fine because of all we accomplished in generating value through R&D.

As the quarters went on, it became obvious that a value-added strategy works in the long term. Short-term, it might be expensive, but in the end you get the payoffs.

In addition to hands-on experience with how a value-added strategy works, the customers gain insight into how important it is for their suppliers to not only meet but anticipate their needs. As Parker noted, "Everything our customers learned during those four days raised their expectations of what they should be getting from FPC." As one can see, inviting customers is, in a very real sense, a way of making a commitment to better customer service.

Module Five: Corporate Culture

Module Five brings the focus inward to FPC's corporate culture, the customers having left the Leadership Institute after the computer simulation. The objective is to develop and apply principles for identifying factors that help or hinder FPC's ability to become a more customer/market-driven enterprise. Participants look at how a corporate culture is shaped and reshaped by vision, power, structure, and resources. They learn how to use leadership skills to generate changes throughout the organization.

Participants report that corporate culture module teaches them how to use analytical tools to carefully probe the culture and renews belief in themselves as leaders, and therefore as change agents. As one executive put it:

If we're going to effect change—and I now know that we can do that—what we need to do is share with our people, all of them, what we're about. For me, that means developing a marketing strategy for molded products and [knowing] how all this ties together.

I have an obligation to both salaried and hourly people to share with them a vision for each business and where we're headed. We need to discuss what barriers they see and take them through some possible solutions. It's important for them to have a sense of ownership in the process. Sure, it's difficult to understand a vision, but if you can get a real dialogue going, you can get everybody moving toward where you need to be.

By the end of Module Five, executives formulated definite, detailed plans for how they would bring the new vision and culture to their units.

A NEW FOCUS

Although it is not a goal of Week Two to increase business with the customers who attend the institute, that is exactly what happened when the program was first offered. During the following months, business with those customers grew significantly and continues to remain very strong. That includes international customers, a rapidly growing market that FPC has been eager to develop more aggressively.

But much more important than what shows up on the scorecard is the new mind-set at Weyerhaeuser Forest Products Company. Intensive communication with customers and prompter, better service to them quickly became a way of life. The new customer focus did not end with attendance at the Leadership Institute. For example, Bingham writes in the 1987 FPC Annual Report:

> During 1987, the amount of time we spent face-to-face with customers reached an all-time high. Hundreds of customers visited our facilities and hundreds of more people took advantage of invitations from customers to visit their operations first-hand.
>
> At Cottage Grove, Oregon, for example, dozens of our production workers from our lumber mill and glulam beam plant visited customers as part of our continuing program to increase our awareness of customers' needs.
>
> . . . This knowledge has enabled us to develop value-added products and services, packaged and promoted in ways appealing to our customers. . . .

Equally impressive is what executives, particularly those not directly involved in marketing, are doing in their own individual units. A follow-up study was conducted in which FPC executives were asked what they were doing differently as a result of attending Week Two of the Leadership Institute.

> One of my roles involves the administrative processing of invoices, bills of lading, systems interface, etc. All of these basic functions are getting much greater emphasis when they interface with customers.

> I now ask the question—how are we making a difference—in product development regarding customer/market needs.

> I put market/customer orientation as the most important selection criterion in hiring a new wood products operations director for the Washington Division. Prior to Week Two, the leading criterion was manufacturing expertise.

I set new quality control standards for products packaging, stenciling, and overall presentation in the division.

I changed the whole emphasis in my group to what we provide—shifted from process to customer needs and interests.

I worked on electronic data links with other functions so that we can build bridges that will tie us together with customers.

I'm spending a lot of time working with the issue of product differentiation and competitive advantage at our two divisions.

To date, no other American corporation has involved customers to the extent that Weyerhaeuser Forest Products Company has. The precedent has been set—and the model launched. Rather than being a threat, customers, as the Weyerhaeuser experience clearly demonstrates, can become genuine partners in helping themselves and their vendors achieve mutual success.

Customers *want* to share their views, expectations, and hopes. The obviousness of that desire—and need—is almost painful to observe. But until corporations open themselves to meeting that need, "getting close to the customer" will remain a nice bit of rhetoric from a book that sold well in 1981. When that rhetoric becomes a widespread reality throughout corporate America, our country will begin to see the long-overdue customer revolution that will change the way we do business—around the world.

VI THE NEW LEADERS

11 LEADERSHIP DEVELOPMENT AT GENERAL FOODS

One of the great debates that has raged for years in executive development circles centers around whether or not leadership can be taught. One camp argues vociferously that it cannot, that leadership is a gift that one is born with and if individuals have not been given that innate attribute, no amount of education or development will give it to them. The other camp argues just as strenuously that leadership can be taught, that there are identifiable skills that can be developed in individuals to make them leaders.

In recent years, the nay-sayers appear to have lost ground. As we have seen, several of America's leading corporate institutions are providing in-depth courses for their senior executives targeted specifically at leadership. This trend is hardly surprising. When asked to identify the areas most critical for their executives, the respondents to our 1988 survey of executive development in Fortune 500 companies ranked leadership in second place—right behind global competitiveness.

John Kotter, chairman of the Organizational Behavior and Human Resource Management Department at the Harvard Business School, finds a direct connection between these two areas. He argues persuasively that the U.S. loss of competitiveness is directly attributable to a lack of corporate leadership. He is highly critical of the "painfully visible examples of senior management teams in certain companies that fail to adapt to new competitive environments, to changing technologies

175

and to global markets." He goes on to suggest that new approaches are needed to foster leadership development.

As we have seen, companies have adopted several different methods of improving leadership skills, incorporating everything from the physical challenge of the outdoor experience to the mental challenge of Socratic discussion. These are powerful ways to improve leadership skills and appear to provide persuasive evidence that leadership *can* be developed. Says one executive development professional: "We are not talking about *teaching* leadership. We are talking about developing it through experience and feedback, and that's an important distinction. Executives have already demonstrated some capacity for leadership or they wouldn't be where they are. We're talking about taking people that have the latent capabilities and helping them develop."

A company that has done one of the best and most sweeping jobs of developing leadership in its executives is General Foods (GF). What follows is a detailed look at the GF approach to leadership development—beginning with its 1983 Business Leadership Program and continuing with its Executive Leadership Program, which is ongoing today.

THE NEW VISION AT GENERAL FOODS

As the 1980s were ushered in, it was clear that General Foods had lost some of its luster. Although the company was still large, growing, and profitable, it had slowly dropped from its position of preeminence among food companies. Competition had intensified. Consumer tastes had changed. And General Foods had not kept pace.

Two forces converged to renew focus on senior management training and development as a key ingredient in returning General Foods to its earlier glory. The first was the personal commitment and style of Philip L. Smith, former president and chief operating officer. According to an associate, Smith, now CEO at Pillsbury, "is a leader in the truest sense of that word. He has clear vision of where he wants to take General Foods, and he considers it a major responsibility of his to articulate that vision to his senior managers. And it goes beyond rhetoric. There is absolutely no gap between his words and his behavior."

Smith brought with him to his new position a reputation as a deep thinker and as someone who believed that leadership can and must be taught in the corporate environment. "I've always been comfortable with the notion," he says, "that leadership skills can be developed and taught, that the business schools have not traditionally considered this part of their charter, and that a company cannot be a superior organization if it does not have superior leaders."

The second force at work at General Foods was the outcome of a study conducted by the professional training and development staff, at Smith's request. Over a period of several weeks, a number of senior executives, officers, and general managers were interviewed to identify current issues and needs regarding leadership. Three main issues emerged:

1. The need to translate the newly adopted corporate mission statement into business actions
2. The need to identify and communicate the parameters of acceptable risk-taking so that executives could be more aggressive and innovative and know that they were still acting within corporate boundaries
3. The need to develop personal leadership behaviors that would support, reinforce, and reward results

Underlying these issues was a belief that senior management must *visibly* demonstrate actions and behavior that would reinforce GF's stated goals of becoming an innovative, aggressive organization responsive to opportunity. Armed with the data from the interviews and with Smith's personal commitment, the professional training and development staff completed a conceptual model for a senior-level management development program.

The Business Leadership Program was based on the GF "vision" of becoming "the premier food and beverage company in the world through providing superior consumer satisfaction." The use of the word *vision*— rather than *goal* or *objective*—is important. A corporate document puts it this way: "The word vision is used because it connotes a personal commitment and focus which can enable others to achieve excellence. To a great extent, it is the ownership, communication and activation of a leadership vision that will enable each business and functional unit to achieve premier status."

THE BUSINESS LEADERSHIP PROGRAM

A big decision made early in the program's development was that it would not deal with leadership in the abstract but would tie leadership very specifically and directly to the business results of General Foods. Leadership, to Phil Smith, "is not essentially something that people study. It is something that people do. It follows from this that leadership is not an innate quality, but a decision. People can *decide* to be leaders; therefore, leadership can be taught, or at least it can be developed."

Five objectives for the program were hammered out. It was agreed that the executives who completed the program would ultimately be able to:

- better identify results that can be achieved by his or her unit or function;
- identify the changes needed in the unit or function's current environment in order to produce superior results;
- recognize—through the feedback of subordinates—his or her personal impact as a leader of the unit or function;
- identify strategies and opportunities for empowering his or her unit or function;
- identify personal actions that reinforce and reward the values and behaviors needed to achieve the goals of the unit or function and, ultimately, of the corporation.

The program ran three and a half days and divided neatly into three segments—*owning* the vision, *communicating* the vision, and *activating* the vision.

Owning the Vision

"Owning the vision" means getting each participant to fully understand, personalize, and internalize what it takes to lead his or her unit or function toward excellence. Each participant spent time alone and in small groups fantasizing about how the company will look and behave when it has achieved its goal of becoming the world's "premier food and beverage company."

Participants were instructed to be specific in their imaging about their unit's environment, their staff, and their business goals and strategies. Most importantly, they rigorously assessed their own strengths and weaknesses as leaders. A worksheet was provided to help focus the imaging.

After discussing in small groups their view of the future, the process was repeated, but with one crucial difference: the focus switched to the

aspirations for their units, and a heavy dose of introspection, participants pinpointed the factors critical to the success of their organization— those actions that would reflect significant movement toward their vision of business excellence. Each executive was asked to initiate and to share the plan with one other person, thereby building commitment and increasing his or her motivation to stick with its implementation.

The reaction to the Business Leadership Program was so positive that, virtually unchanged, the program was conducted monthly. Phil Smith felt confident, based on the reactions of participants, that managers were really excited about the program and felt that it was very beneficial. He noted that "people are thinking about and talking about leadership . . . and specifically, about their own leadership style, where it needs to improve and how it can be improved."

Smith was surprised to learn "the degree to which the elements of what the company is about and doing are really not understood at all." He felt that they had communicated these things effectively in the past, but apparently they had failed. Through his involvement in the Business Leadership Program, he had an opportunity to reinforce the vision of the company. He also found that the program was an excellent way for participants to actually internalize the mission and other aspects of the vision of the company. Eventually, all of GF's 350 most senior executives completed the course.

THE EXECUTIVE LEADERSHIP PROGRAM

Shortly after the Business Leadership Program had been delivered to the targeted audience, a survey was conducted for the top forty officers at General Foods. This group had been excluded from participation in the seminar. "The survey results," says one insider, "confirmed what a lot of us already suspected. Leadership skills like coaching and counseling were not widely used and understood at the very top of the house and needed attention."

"That survey," says Bassin, "gave us a lot of ammunition. So did the success of Business Leadership. But two other events also intervened that caused us to get serious about developing leadership at the officer level of the organization."

The first was the acquisition of General Foods by Philip Morris and the resulting reorganization of the company into two large business sectors—one for domestic operations and the other for international.

New management teams were assembled, and there was a critical need for team-building.

The second factor was Phil Smith's growing awareness of the power of leadership. "He had always been way out in front of the organization on his appreciation of leadership," says Bassin, "but the more we got into it, the more deeply he understood its enormous impact, and the more convinced he became that it could be taught."

The depth of Smith's conviction comes through in his own words:

> I have been discussing the importance of leadership within General Foods for several years now and it has taken on a very personal meaning for me. I see leadership as the foundation for all growth—as individuals and as a company. In my judgment, leadership is the single most important element in moving an organization and its people to peak performance. Without superior leadership, peak performance is highly unlikely.

Smith also believes that leadership is an evolving pursuit that one must constantly struggle with. "As people and the world change and/or new needs and challenges arise," he says, "so do the challenges of leadership. It does not exist in a vacuum; it impacts and is impacted by an ever-changing context."

The outcome of Smith's thinking was the development and implementation of the General Foods Executive Leadership Program—one of the best of its kind in industry. It consists of five phases spread over an eighteen-month period and occupies about twenty days of a participant's time. Over the eighteen-month period, that amounts to about 5 percent of an officer's time—a significant chunk for a senior executive.

Its primary purpose is to "promote individual growth and development, that is, general broadening, including the ability to better appreciate and utilize diversity." Within that framework, the program has five objectives:

1. To identify key organization values, beliefs, and attitudes and their corresponding leadership practices
2. To increase self-awareness of achievement strengths/weaknesses and their impact on the organization
3. To deepen the appreciation for teamwork and diversity
4. To provide models of leadership through self-directed learning and ongoing dialogue with GF peers
5. To provide a basis for making significant contributions to GF or to the GF community

The program is designed for a small group of around fifteen people. Ideally, the fifteen people move through all five phases as a team or class. A question that often arises about the eighteen-month period is why it takes so long. Bassin has a ready and convincing answer.

We chose such a long time frame because we know that real growth requires sufficient time, particularly for adults. Since this type of intensive experience presents such an ideal opportunity for team-building, we made this a secondary explicit outcome. Team-building doesn't happen overnight either, and that's why we settled on the long time frame. This type of development experience just wouldn't happen in a concentrated period.

Phase One: Humanities and Intellectual Broadening

This is the most controversial and unusual phase. Its objectives are twofold:

- To enhance participants' understanding of their own basic values, the organization's values, and the relationship of these to leading the business
- To promote an appreciation for risk-taking and a commitment to excellence, judgment, creativity, and diversity.

General Foods pursues these objectives by having a local university provide a three-day "theater-based multidimensional experience of the humanities." According to Marc Bassin:

The purpose of the theater experience was to enhance . . . participants' understanding of their own basic values and the relationship of these to leading the business. We purposely chose theater as the medium because of its capacity to force participation, interaction, and introspection. We wanted to stay away from case studies or other areas of comfortability for the participants, such as simulations or readings. We worked closely with a university to bring together a small group of actors and actresses and a marvelous theatrical historian. We took the group off-site for three days and focused the experience around two plays, Shakespeare's *Henry the Fourth* and O'Neill's *Long Day's Journey into Night*.

The participants viewed key scenes acted out for them by the actors and actresses. (They had previously been given the plays to read.) They were then asked to break into small groups and to create skits for each other to express thoughts and feelings about what they were experiencing.

According to Bassin,

> One of the skits very cleverly depicted the gap between our rhetoric and behavior. Shortly thereafter the participants watched the Tyrone family fall apart before their very eyes because no one took action when there were so many opportunities to do so. Using Shakespeare's main characters from *Henry the Fourth,* to represent different leadership philosophies, a critical discussion followed about what kind of leadership and change GF needed from this group. This turned into an "evolution versus revolution" debate. . . .
>
> This theater experience was very controversial. It exposed problems with General Foods, and differing philosophies in an as yet ununited group of key officers, about how to proceed. Nevertheless, many of the participants began to more fully appreciate the power of using images and emotions, versus words and numbers, to communicate critical messages. Using this new understanding, they broke into three groups to present images of what this team might become, resulting in one very emotionally moving demonstration in which a group worked *together* to create a burning torch, a new symbol of togetherness.

The theater experience clearly had impact. Some participants were frustrated and disturbed, unsure of why they were doing this or where it was leading. For others, new ways to communicate were explored and major needs were identified, around both of which a team and a shared approach to change could be built. The theater experience clearly established the need and laid the groundwork for Phase Two.

Phase Two: Team-building

Phase Two of the program is aimed at team development and centers around an outdoor experience. It has four objectives:

1. To enhance self-awareness as an individual, team member, and leader
2. To facilitate team development
3. To "lift the cap" to enhance creativity
4. To initiate discussions for team projects

Teams were encouraged to develop their own team-building activity and to choose from among four outdoor options:

1. A five-day program that includes indoor and outdoor activities, creative problem-solving, and a team wilderness experience
2. A seven-day program that includes sailing, expeditioning, swimming, running, and climbing and is geared toward "individual performance enhancement, leadership, the maintenance of focus in the face of obstacles, productive handling of stress and the dynamics of the creative process"
3. A three-day mountaineering and river rafting experience
4. A "changing the game" program aimed at development, mutual support, creativity, hidden personal resources, learning, and leadership. Participants worked outdoors but slept indoors during the three-day program.

A Personal Account.   GF's Marc Bassin participated personally and is uniquely qualified to describe what happened with his team from a firsthand perspective. He graciously agreed to provide this account, which we include here at some length.

"The purpose of Phase Two of the Executive Leadership Program was simple and straightforward: team-building. It was clear from Phase One that Erv's [Erv Shane, president of the U.S. Grocery Business Sector of General Foods] staff was far from being a cohesive team. The general managers viewed themselves as independent business leaders who happened to report in to an entity called a sector. Without a strong sense of purpose and trust, communication was guarded, cooperation was minimal, and joint problem-solving almost nonexistent. Erv believed that the U.S. Grocery Business Sector could not continue to function in this manner. At a minimum, development opportunities and resources had to be shared across the business units. And from our theater experience, it was clear that a growing consensus was emerging that a radical transformation was needed across the entire sector if we were to be successful in the future. Erv believed that this group, his staff, had to become a more cohesive team if it was to lead this type of change.

"With the help of an external resource, we designed and implemented our team experience. Erv's staff members were told that they would be involved in three days of physical activities together, performing tasks and exercises, which would provide an opportunity to examine and improve the way they worked together. Simultaneously, this type of physical activity would give them all a chance to interact, communicate, and get to know each other on a much deeper and more personal level.

"It was clear from Erv that he expected their full participation. The staff had no other information about the types of activities except what to wear and where to go. The good news for the staff was that we would be sleeping in comfortable accommodations and that the activities would be neither life-threatening nor inordinately physically rigorous. With that as background, coupled with a great deal of anxiety and an equally stimulating sense of excitement, we began what was to become a breakthrough experience for the group."

Loosening Up. "I knew we were off to a decent start when I heard everyone actually shouting. We had begun by forming a circle to do 'loosening-up' exercises. This was very foreign to them, while everyone complied, some were clearly uncomfortable. The first moment of truth came when everyone was asked to shout individually, one after the other, as part of these exercises. Feeble though some shouts were, everyone participated, and we began to build momentum from there. What followed was a series of physical tasks, all requiring teamwork, planning, and execution. In all cases, successful completion required cooperation and interdependence. The tasks became progressively harder, requiring more problem-solving, experimentation, creativity, and the ability to learn from failure.

"Often subgroups were required to complete critical components of a task. Time limits were imposed, and in all cases the leadership and resources necessary to complete the tasks had to emerge from the group. An early exercise involved getting each member of the team through a 'spider's web' of rope without touching any of the ropes and never passing an individual through the same hole twice. A more complex task involved constructing a vehicle out of barrels and boards to cross a particular terrain and then using a swinging rope to cross another area. After each activity (and at designated times during an activity), the group had an opportunity to 'debrief' its progress and examine how well it was working. It was at these points that parallels to the staff's 'back home' work style were explicitly compared and contrasted. Most importantly, these debriefings provided opportunities for the group to experiment with new types of behavior. A number of individuals got the opportunity to play leadership roles, and the emerging skills, strengths, and abilities of the various members were put to better use. The tasks were difficult, and the group failed to complete a number of them. Here was an opportunity to learn from failure and use this to move forward.

"Before long it was crystal clear to the group that the same patterns of behavior that characterized their work and interaction back home emerged in these tasks. It was also very clear that some of these patterns were plainly dysfunctional. For example, the staff always seemed to get hung up in the planning phase with too many people spending too much time in that activity. As the tasks progressed, the group was able to move more quickly to action through directive leadership, more differentiation of roles, and better communication. This same issue, a preoccupation with planning versus a bias toward action, was one of the behaviors Erv was most interested in changing in his sector. As the staff experienced the positive effects on completing tasks in this new manner, this became a much more deeply held and commonly shared goal."

The Ropes.   "Day Two was spent 'on the ropes.' Here the output was slightly different, an opportunity to experience firsthand the relationship between risk-taking and support. The ropes course was a series of ropes sixty feet above the group tied securely across huge trees. There were a variety of ways up to various platforms, a variety of traverses [ways to cross] and a variety of ways down. The idea was simple: each person would decide what he/she wanted to do, choose the degree of challenge (risk) with which he/she was comfortable, and share those goals with his/her teammates (we were organized into teams of three). We were then taught how to physically assist each person on the course— feeding out rope on their lifelines, spotting, guiding, encouraging, etc.

"For many of the staff, confronting the ropes was an extremely traumatic experience. In the hours that followed, all of us learned a great deal about risk-taking and support. With sweat, hugs, some tears, and a great deal of shouting and encouragement, individuals found that with human contact and support they could do or help others do that which they thought not possible. This became particularly clear to all of us when one of the staff found himself frozen up in the air clinging to a tree. We were all up there with him, our hearts in our throats, sweating and terrified (although always knowing that he was perfectly safe—tied in). No matter how hard he tried, he could not get himself to move across the ropes. All of a sudden, Dave of the staff climbed up to a platform across from him and by having him 'look at my eyes,' guided him across. The human, personal contact, the trust and belief that make up the support necessary for real risk-taking, was there before our eyes, for all of us to see and touch. None of us will ever forget what we learned about risk-taking and support from the ropes. All of us vowed to incorporate it into the new team that was emerging."

The Wall. "The final physical activity of this experience was the wall. This exercise required getting everyone over a 13-foot wall in a given time period. As usual, our group stood around planning and wasting time until Erv finally said, 'Enough, Bill, get your ass over the wall.' Bill ran, leaped up, grabbed the top, and hoisted himself up and over. With that surge of action, the whole staff quickly threw and dragged each other over the wall. The wall became a critical image of action and cooperation for the staff as it worked together planning the transformation of the sector over the next few months.

"Day Three was spent in more debriefing, in making plans to apply the lessons we had learned directly to the workplace. A highlight was the invitation by Erv for this group to become a sector 'board of directors' that would work as a team to lead the U.S. Grocery Business Sector into the nineties. The staff agenda had radically changed, from a group of individual business heads to an emerging team with a purpose. Remembering the power of images from the theater experience, the staff developed such an image to describe its transformation. It would be like a 'baseball team,' where each person must not only play his/her position but must also contribute to the team by backing up and helping his/her teammates if the team was to be a winner.

"This phase clearly provided a major breakthrough for the staff. They had redefined themselves with a purpose. They had committed themselves to working in new and more efficient ways. Individuals knew each other much more intimately and felt much more comfortable with each other. Communication had greatly improved, and the group now had a commonly shared metaphor for what it wanted to be and how to get there. Their energy was up, and they were clearly a different and stronger group than when they had started."

Phase Three: Self-assessment

The primary purpose of this phase is to better enable each individual to understand his or her own areas of strength and weakness so as to more effectively determine personal development goals through an intensive self-assessment experience. Each individual filled out a series of self-assessment instruments. The assessment was quite extensive, incorporating into a comprehensive profile what individuals thought about themselves, feedback from peers and subordinates, and data from a series of in-depth psychological tests. Group sessions were used to prepare individuals to fully understand and utilize their assessments. Each individual also had a personal one-to-one session with a psychologist to review his or her profile and forge development plans.

Again, Marc Bassin notes:

> In addition to personal assessment, the group also had an opportunity to examine its "group profile." This proved to be particularly revealing, since the dominant group tendencies were so consistent with the behavior the group had begun to discuss in the first two phases. Benefiting from the openness the group had gained during its team-building experience, a critical discussion followed about achievement. How did planning effect achievement, and were we doing our business planning in a way that was helping or hindering us? The group concluded that our tendency to overplan and promise was generating a cycle of self-defeating behavior, which was resulting in both poor business performance and poor morale. The group there and then made a resolution to begin a new cycle of "realistic planning" and to change whatever else it would take to reshape the sector so that we could achieve our agreed-upon business goals.

This group's resolution led naturally into its Phase Four project, which it called "Project Achievement."

Phase Four: The Renewal Project

This phase had two objectives:

1. To contribute either to organizational renewal and the achievement of corporate vision or to the broader GF community
2. To integrate and synthesize individual learning in a team activity of importance to the organization

Although four months are designated for this phase, it is actually an open-ended process. Marc Bassin explains why.

"While we always had great expectations for this phase, we never expected it to emerge into an undertaking of such magnitude as the transformation of the sector. About nine months after the beginning of the program, General Foods was decentralized into three independent operating companies. Erv and his staff therefore used Project

Achievement as a critical part of the foundation for building the new U.S. Grocery Company.

"In the new company, business development will be done quite differently. Using what he learned from the theater experience, Erv chose to communicate the difference through what has now become known as the 'boat experience.' This involves building a raft out of 50-gallon drums, two-by-fours, and rope. Once built, 'development teams' have to paddle it across a lake to capture various colored flags symbolizing new products or development opportunities.

"Erv took his entire staff through this experience. This involved two attempts. In the first, the traditional General Foods style was used. The team was given vague goals followed by a series of nit-picking, process-laden, unhelpful, and time-consuming requirements. For example, each team was required to write a plan detailing construction of the raft and role utilization before it could launch. These plans were 'not accepted' by management and required modification. Working the old way, Erv's staff was unable to retrieve the flags in the allotted time frame. In fact, one raft capsized, sending everyone overboard. Then the staff went through the exercise again following the new approach. This was characterized by precise goals laid out at the beginning (such as which flags were most valuable) and no meddling about how to proceed from management above.

"The result—success. Both teams (Erv's staff was divided into two teams) retrieved the flags in the allotted time, learning was shared between the teams, and most importantly, management provided help and assistance to the teams when requested to do so by them."

Phase Five: Peer Leadership

This phase has two primary objectives:

1. To provide an opportunity for modeling teaching and coaching behaviors
2. To broaden the executive's knowledge and experience by examining in depth an issue of significant personal relevance.

This phase has not yet been implemented. Says Bassin: "We are currently planning to devote portions of our off-site quarterly meetings to this 'peer-teaching' process. The peer-teaching activity is an attempt to institutionalize the development process by placing the responsibility for ongoing growth squarely in the hands of the individual executive. We believe it will prove to be a simple, effective, and exciting mechanism for this purpose."

Each executive will be responsible for identifying an important leadership issue and for presenting it to his or her peers. Executives may choose to do this any way they want—as a lecture and discussion or as a panel presentation, for example.

"It's even conceivable," says Bassin, "that a venturesome executive would like to turn his or her issue into a drama experience or an outdoor experience. It will be interesting to see just how far they go."

INDIVIDUAL AND CORPORATE GROWTH

It is too early to determine what the full impact of the GF Executive Leadership Program will eventually be. But it is just as clear that it is already having a substantial impact. "What is most evident," says Bassin, "is the impact it is having on the way we think about leadership and development as a primary intervention for transforming an entire organization. . . . The goal has always been to create a vision, an excitement, and active commitment for growth among individuals at the top of the organization so that this behavior can indeed cascade down."

There is ample evidence that this is happening. Many GF executives and managers have now had the "boat experience." At least fifteen groups have been on various outdoor experiences. Several task forces—similar to the one that designed the boat experience—have been established. Perhaps most important, Project Achievement continues to work toward establishing a foundation for the new U.S. Grocery Company.

What advice would Bassin pass on to other companies grappling with how to go about leadership development? Here are a few of his pearls of wisdom:

- "Accept the premise that leadership can be developed. Our experience proves it."
- "Approach it as an ongoing journey, not a short-term objective. It's a process with no discernible end."
- "Nontraditional approaches—particularly outdoor experiences— can be powerful development tools."
- "Be willing to accept some failures. If you're on the cutting edge and charting new waters, you are bound to make some mistakes."

- "Make sure you have top-level commitment—not just the endorsement, but commitment in the truest and fullest sense of the word."
- "Be prepared for change. It will manifest itself in ways you would never expect."

A case in point was an impromptu meeting held in the GF courtyard at which Erv Shane spoke to some 2000 people about the changes the company was going through. Why not through the traditional General Foods memo or house organ?

"Because," says Shane, "memos just don't move the heart and the soul. I learned this in the theater experience."

12 FOR CEOs ONLY: USE EXECUTIVE DEVELOPMENT TO COMPETITIVE ADVANTAGE

In many large corporations, as we have seen in this book, the executive education function has risen to the competitive challenges of the 1980s. It is important to note, however, that executive development professionals have not done so alone. Where executive education efforts have been successful, these professionals have had a willing and proactive partnership with the CEO.

This partnership has tended to develop in one of two ways. Either the CEO conceives of a way in which executive education can help achieve business objectives and direct the human resource professionals to start a program, or the human resource people conceive of the idea and sell it to the CEO. When it happens in the latter way, executive education is effective only when the CEO truly "buys in to" the idea and *actively* supports it in deeds as well as words. In other words, unless the CEO is really supporting executive education, it cannot and does not play a central and stategic role in the corporation.

When this partnership between the CEO and the executive education function exists, executive education can have enormous impact. The following are some of the more common purposes to which executive education is being put by corporations today.

COMMON OBJECTIVES OF
EXECUTIVE EDUCATION

One objective for executive education is *establishing organizational identity*. Thus, the objective of General Electric's chairman and CEO in the 1950s, Ralph J. Cordiner, in establishing the Management Development Institute was to transform individual employees into members of the GE family. Although the GE of today is a vastly different company, today's chairman and CEO, Jack Welch, uses the institute in much the same way. "A key objective," Welch says, "is to get my managers and executives to identify with the organization, to understand its values and strategies, and to get them to buy into General Electric."

A second objective for executive education is *developing a shared vision and unity of purpose*. A good example of this is the work done by Philip Smith while he was CEO at General Foods. "One of the things we found out early on in developing a program on leadership for our executives," he says, "was that you cannot expect them to lead in a vacuum. A fundamental of leadership is a vision—a shared vision of where you want to lead. So when we started our Business Leadership Program, we based it on the General Foods vision of becoming the premier food and beverage company in the world through providing superior consumer satisfaction."

A third typical objective for executive education is *communicating and implementing corporate strategy*. David Kearns did this particularly well when he took over as CEO at Xerox. Faced with intense competition from the Japanese, Kearns needed to revamp the corporation's strategic direction and make sure his entire management team agreed and understood where they were heading.

Not only did he need to get his entire management team to understand the strategy, but he needed to obtain their commitment to implementing it and making it happen in the real world. He wanted each executive to understand his or her role in implementation. "I also had to energize them," he says, "to make the corporate strategy their strategy. . . . I had to communicate our direction for the rest of the 1980s and get everyone on board."

A fourth executive education objective is *shaping, managing, and if necessary, modifying a culture*. That's precisely what Des Hudson did as CEO of Northern Telecom. He inherited a team of managers who had come to NTI from a wide variety of other corporations and had brought widely differing values and management principles with them. "Molding a disjointed group of bright, capable managers into a team," says Hudson, "was a high priority. I had a limited window of opportunity and had to move quickly to establish and communicate a common culture. Frankly, our executive education program is the only vehicle I know of that could have made this happen as quickly and as effectively."

A fifth and very common objective for executive education is *developing critical attitudes, knowledge, and skills*. When divestiture led to the creation of BellSouth as an independent company, John Clendenin, chairman and CEO, knew he needed to prepare his managers up and down the line for the rigors of competition. From virtually a standing start, he created the BellSouth Management Institute and developed a state-of-the-art curriculum. Says Clendenin: "This was an important piece in our strategy to become more competitive and to bring our executives and managers into this mind-set. In many ways we viewed it as an investment."

A sixth objective of executive education is *identifying and addressing key business issues*. At Motorola, the key business issue was nothing short of the survival of the company. Motorola's markets were being ravaged by some very formidable competitors in the Far East. Robert Galvin, chairman and CEO, realized that if Motorola did not rally to the challenge, it would quite possibly cease to exist as a corporate entity.

Galvin used executive education to help his senior team understand the nature and the extent of the competitive threat represented by the Far East. Says Galvin:

> American business—and Motorola people are no exception—doesn't fully understand the scope and the nature of global competitiveness. The intensity and the quality of the threat from Asia is underestimated and misunderstood. We've been thinking and talking about Japan for years, but we never really zeroed in on the nature of the threat and what our strategic response ought to be. Executive education helped us do that.

Now, Motorola's executive education strategy has the top 200 executives annually attending similar programs, each of which addresses the most critical business issue facing the company.

A seventh objective is *building teamwork and networks*. Charles Bingham, president of the Weyerhaeuser Forest Products Company, used executive education for precisely this objective. He wanted to get all his senior people from different parts of the organization pulling together as one team—helping each other and creating synergy. He used executive development to do it. At the Leadership Institute, people from different functions at different locations came together—sometimes for the first time. At the same time, Bingham was supplying his executives with the knowledge, skills, and attitudes needed to transform and revitalize the organization into a customer/market-driven competitive force.

An eighth objective of executive development is *providing a forum for management communication*—both vertical and horizontal. Several CEOs have confided to me that they are often frustrated by their inability to elicit candid discussion from their senior team. "It's understandable," says one, "They're all jockeying for position and don't want to be the messenger who gets killed. But understandable or not, it's frustrating." Executive education forums—because they are usually offsite and informal and put a premium on open discussion—can break through barriers that normally interfere with candor. As described in the preceding chapters, any number of CEOs use these programs to get honest presentations from participants on what can be done to improve corporate performance.

They also use them for downward communication. Many CEOs have used executive education programs as platforms to communicate corporate strategies, to articulate their vision, to underscore corporate values and priorities, and to motivate their management teams around key issues.

Communication among program participants is also crucial. In addition to building the working relationships and networks that are essential to getting things done in an organization, these opportunities for sharing ideas and experiences—that is, learning from each other—are valuable. Also beneficial is the identification of ways to collaborate as a team in bringing ideas, products, and services to the marketplace.

A *ninth* objective is *enabling a management team to understand the need for careful planning before action.* Emhart is a good case in point. CEO T. Mitchel Ford wanted to develop a rational approach to developing Emhart into a global competitor. His senior management team saw the opportunities, but wanted to forge ahead in a somewhat unfocused fashion. Ford used executive education to broaden their perspective and make them aware of not only the opportunities in going global but also the pitfalls.

Lastly, a tenth objective is *improving leadership.* The programs at BellSouth, Weyerhaeuser, and General Foods are probably the best examples in this book of using education to develop leadership. Says GF's Smith: "Leadership is the most basic means we have for moving the business ahead. In its highest form, it creates a sense of destiny for the organization and makes clear the role each of us must play in achieving it. To be effective at this, leaders of GF must be actively and visibly engaged in their own personal growth. Corporate executive education programs are one way to achieve this growth."

FROM INDIVIDUAL DEVELOPMENT TO STRATEGIC TOOL

The executive education programs described in this book provide ample testimony to the fact that these programs work. It is little wonder that a number of recent studies have found that senior executives perceive executive development programs as a key competitive advantage, right up there with product quality, innovation, and cost containment.

For instance, our 1988 study of selected Fortune 500 companies found that the top managers—CEOs, presidents, COOs—are increasingly willing to invest their own time in shaping development programs that focus on leadership, implementation of strategy, becoming customer/market-focused, managing organizational change, total quality control, and so on.

That represented a distinct shift: respondents indicated that the topics emphasized in the previous three to five years were, in descending order, financial management, general management skills, leadership, communication skills, implementation of business strategies, and total quality control. As one can see, leadership and strategic issues grew in importance; customer orientation, not among the top five formerly, became the third most important issue.

There is no mistaking it: executive education has come out of the closet and taken its place on center stage. This transformation has moved executive education from its *traditional* role to a *strategic* role. As Figure 12–1 indicates, these shifts fall into four categories.

First, there has been a shift in the *purpose* of executive development. Traditionally, it was viewed as a way of developing *individuals* by preparing them for future assignments and broadening their perspectives. In its strategic role, executive development is seen as a vehicle to help the *organization* achieve its strategic objectives; the individual is developed in support of organizational goals. These are, of course, very different purposes. In the past, executive development programs were loose and "nice to do." Now, they are focused and tied to improving corporate performance.

Figure 12-1.   Strategic Executive Development.

	TRADITIONAL	STRATEGIC

PURPOSE	• Develop the Individual
	  – Prepare for Future
	    Assignments
	  – Broaden
	    Persepctives
	  – General Business
	    Focus
		• Help Reach Vision/
		  Achieve Strategic
		  Objectives
		  – Improve Individual
		    and Organizational
		    Performance
		  – Build Unity of
		    Purpose
		  – Identify/Address
		    Business Issues

CONTENT	• Mini-MBA	• Company Specific
		• Competencies
		  Needed to Achieve
		  Strategic Objectives

METHODS	• Lecture/Discussion Case Method	• Experiential/Workshop
PARTICIPANTS	• Middle to Upper Management	• Executives

Second, the *content* of executive education programs has shifted. Traditionally, these programs were rather conceptual and generic and resembled mini-MBA programs: a little finance, a little marketing, and a dash of human resources. No more. The emphasis now is on programs designed for the unique needs of the individual organization. Their content is geared toward the development of the capabilities needed to achieve specific strategic objectives.

Third, the *methods* used to deliver this content have also changed. Traditionally, executive education programs centered around lectures and case studies. Today's executive is more likely to be exposed to workshops, business simulations, outdoor experiences, and a wide variety of other experiential learning. The clear emphasis is on learning by doing.

Fourth, the *participants* themselves have changed. A decade ago, the terms *executive development* or *executive education* were misnomers to some extent. The emphasis was really more on *management* training and development. This, too, has shifted. Although middle- and upper-level managers still receive their share of education attention, they have been joined in the classroom by senior executives.

Not all corporate executive education programs, of course, have made this transition from the traditional role to the strategic. In our experience, there is a very simple reason why. Most of today's CEOs are products of the traditional approach. That's all they have ever been exposed to, and until they come to understand the possibilities and opportunities the new strategic approach represents, they cannot appreciate it. Says one: "It was like a light bulb going on for me when I finally got the message that executive education can be a powerful strategic tool. Once I got the message—once that light bulb went on—the rest was relatively easy."

KEYS TO SUCCESS

There are nine common denominators that separate the programs that are successful from those that are not:

- *Senior management involvement.* In most successful programs, the impetus for executive education comes from the CEO. In all successful programs, the CEO is intimately involved in program design and implementation.
- *Steering/design committees.* These are typically joint committees of senior line executives, human resource professionals, and outside consultants.
- *Thorough research and analysis.* Sometimes called a "needs analysis," this type of research determines what the unique challenges and needs of the corporation are and how they can be met through executive education.
- *Customized, innovative, and integrated program design.* The best programs not only meet the unique needs of the corporation but are integrated into the mainstream of the industry.
- *Implementation that fits.* A good program not only reflects but strengthens the strategy, objectives, issues, culture, and style of the corporation.
- *Real-world orientation.* Executive education programs should be practical and relevant to the executive.
- *Top-notch faculty.* These are the ones who are willing and able to deal with the unique needs of the audience and adapt his or her material accordingly.
- *Experiential learning with an emphasis on participation.* Hands-on involvement and small groups facilitate learning by doing.

- *Focus on back-home application.* The attitude is: "This is *not* a classroom exercise; you are expected to put this information and these new skills to work for the corporation."

Of all of these keys to success, the first one—the active involvement of the CEO—is of paramount importance. We are keenly aware of the demands that are placed upon today's CEO, as well as of the fact that every function feels that the CEO's personal involvement is key to its success. Nevertheless, if today's CEO wants the benefits that executive education offers, he or she must be willing to make the investment of personal time.

CRITICAL QUESTIONS FOR THE CEO

Executive education is not a panacea, however, and it's not right for every CEO in every organization. Before a CEO takes the plunge, he or she would do well to look squarely in the mirror and ask some tough questions:

- Have I set a clear strategic direction for my company? Unless and until the corporation's strategy has been at least broadly articulated and defined, executive development cannot be properly aligned with strategic objectives and such programs could be premature, wasteful, and counterproductive. On the other hand, these programs can be helpful as a way of involving executives in formulating and shaping the vision and strategy.
- Am I committed to seriously using executive development as one way to strengthen my corporation? Halfway measures, off-the-shelf programs, training that is cosmetic in nature, are all doomed to failure in today's world of hard results.
- Am I willing to listen to the recommendations generated by my senior management team, take them seriously, and act upon them as appropriate? A real payoff from the programs described in this book is the development of unity of purpose. The entire management team can be motivated to adopt mutually understood and agreed on objectives.
- Am I willing to invest my time and energy in participating in the design and implementation of the program? If the answer is no, the executive development program is probably not worth doing.

- Am I willing to participate in the entire program? Some CEOs actually feel that they don't personally need these development experiences. Nevertheless, to optimize the potential impact, they must demonstrate their commitment by attending side by side with their executives as full participants.

This last point is critical, yet often given short shrift. A CEO's nonattendance at an executive education program sends a powerful, negative message that can be interpreted in one of two ways. It communicates that either the CEO does not really believe in the value of the program or the CEO "knows it all" and feels that he is above it all. In other words, his senior management team needs what the executive education program has to offer, but the CEO already possesses this information and these skills. Either way, lack of attendance by the CEO is damaging, usually even fatal.

On the other hand, the personal attendance and participation of the CEO sends a powerful, positive message. It communicates to the entire organization that learning is a lifelong process and that all people in the corporation—up to and including the CEO himself—need to continually retool themselves for the challenges of their jobs. If you expect your executives to continually hone their skills to face the challenges posed by rapid change and competition, you certainly should do so as well.

Those challenges—particularly for senior executives—are accelerating at an alarming rate. Competition is likely to become even tougher as more and more developing nations enter the global economy and take their places beside the Japans and the South Koreas. Technology is advancing so rapidly that it's almost impossible to keep up with it. Governments around the world are likely to continue to spin a web of laws, regulations, added-value demands, and tariffs, which the modern executive will need to cope with. Issues of the environment, pay equity, and cross-cultural and cross-national concerns will surface and force new and more complex questions on senior executives.

The list goes on. The point is clear. The challenges facing the modern executive are great and getting greater. It's clear that executive development can help address those challenges. If you can answer yes to the questions posed to CEO's on the preceding pages then you are poised to use executive development as a strategic weapon of your business.

I encourage you to read other chapters of this book that strike your fancy. You'll clearly see how other CEO's are successfully using executive development as a key driver for leading and shaping their organizations and equipping their executives with the attitudes, perspectives, know-how and skills needed to meet and beat the competition as well as lead their enterprises confidently into the 21st century.

INDEX

ABOUT THE AUTHOR

James F. Bolt is founder and president of Executive Development Associates (EDA), a consulting firm specializing in the use of executive development to help achieve strategic objectives and change. EDA develops customized in-company executive education programs and conferences and consults on strategies and processes for executive education, succession planning, and the development of high-potential managers.

Prior to founding EDA in 1982, Mr. Bolt was with Xerox Corporation for sixteen years. As corporate director of Human Resource Planning and Development, he had companywide responsibility for executive education, management training, executive succession planning, human resource planning, employment, and quality-of-work-life activities. Earlier in his Xerox career, he held several key line and staff marketing positions.

Mr. Bolt is the author of numerous articles, having contributed to the *Harvard Business Review, Business Horizons, New Management,* the *Human Resource Planning Journal,* and *Management Review.* His article "Job Security: An Idea Whose Time Has Come," published in the *Harvard Business Review* in November–December 1983, was recognized by the McKinsey Foundation for Management Research as one of the best articles in 1983.

Executive Development: A Strategy for Corporate Competitiveness is Mr. Bolt's first book; it is based on his fifteen years of experience in executive development, including his firm's consulting work with such leading organizations as AT&T, BellSouth Corporation, Coca-Cola, Exxon, General Electric Company, General Motors, Johnson & Johnson, Kodak, Motorola, Northern Telecom, Weyerhaeuser Company, and Xerox Corporation.

Executive Development Associates headquarters is located at 18 Kings Highway North, Westport, Connecticut 06880 (203-226-0672). Executive Development Associates' services are provided in Canada through Executive Development Western, located in Toronto, Ontario (416-362-6863) and Vancouver, British Columbia (604-687-0391).